"If you're a word nut like I am, you'll be a fervent—not a fervid!—fan of Rod Evans's invaluable guide to the most easily confused words in English. I paged through it with zest and zeal—which, if I may spoil the ending, turn out to be not quite the same thing."

    —Ken Jennings, author of *Brainiac: Adventures in the Curious, Competitive, Compulsive World of Trivia Buffs* and holder of the longest winning streak on *Jeopardy!*

"Because the English language possesses far more words than any other, Rod Evans's *The Artful Nuance* is an especially useful reference book for all of us who desire to speak and write right."

    —Richard Lederer, author of *Anguished English*

"A valuable and edifying reference for anyone who is interested in the myriad nuances of our language."

    —Tyler Hinman, four-time American Crossword Puzzle Tournament winner

"Everyone who writes or speaks for a living—or aspires to do so—should read this book! It has something to teach even the most language-savvy among us—from big distinctions to nuggets of nuance. If you don't know the difference between *naked* and *nude*, and *rebut* and *refute*, then this book should be a permanent part of your library."

    —Merl Reagle, syndicated crossword puzzle constructor

"Good communication starts with an effective use of language. Evans presents with crystal clarity distinctions any outstanding students, writers, or speakers would want to be able to use in their everyday world."

    —Joe Edley, three-time American National Scrabble champion and coauthor of *Everything Scrabble*

THE

Artful Nuance

A Refined Guide to
Imperfectly Understood Words
in the English Language

ROD L. EVANS, PH.D.

A Perigee Book

A PERIGEE BOOK
Published by the Penguin Group
Penguin Group (USA) Inc.
375 Hudson Street, New York, New York 10014, USA

Penguin Group (Canada), 90 Eglinton Avenue East, Suite 700, Toronto,
Ontario M4P 2Y3, Canada (a division of Pearson Penguin Canada Inc.)
Penguin Books Ltd., 80 Strand, London WC2R 0RL, England
Penguin Group Ireland, 25 St. Stephen's Green, Dublin 2, Ireland
(a division of Penguin Books Ltd.)
Penguin Group (Australia), 250 Camberwell Road, Camberwell, Victoria 3124, Australia
(a division of Pearson Australia Group Pty. Ltd.)
Penguin Books India Pvt. Ltd., 11 Community Centre, Panchsheel Park,
New Delhi—110 017, India
Penguin Group (NZ), 67 Apollo Drive, Rosedale, North Shore 0632, New Zealand
(a division of Pearson New Zealand Ltd.)
Penguin Books (South Africa) (Pty.) Ltd., 24 Sturdee Avenue, Rosebank,
Johannesburg 2196, South Africa

Penguin Books Ltd., Registered Offices: 80 Strand, London WC2R 0RL, England

While the author has made every effort to provide accurate telephone numbers and Internet addresses at the time of publication, neither the publisher nor the author assumes any responsibility for errors, or for changes that occur after publication. Further, the publisher does not have any control over and does not assume any responsibility for author or third-party websites or their content.

Copyright © 2009 by Rod Evans
Cover design by Elizabeth Sheehan
Text design by Tiffany Estreicher

First edition: February 2009

Library of Congress Cataloging-in-Publication Data

Evans, Rod L., 1956–
   The artful nuance : a refined guide to imperfectly understood words in the English language / Rod L. Evans.
      p. cm.
   "A Perigee Book."
   Includes bibliographical references.
   ISBN 978-0-399-53482-9
   1. English language—Usage—Dictionaries.   2. English language—Terms and phrases.
3. Vocabulary.   I. Title.
   PE1464.A78 2009
   428.1—dc22   2008034651

PRINTED IN THE UNITED STATES OF AMERICA

10 9 8 7 6 5 4 3 2 1

Most Perigee books are available at special quantity discounts for bulk purchases for sales promotions, premiums, fund-raising, or educational use. Special books, or book excerpts, can also be created to fit specific needs. For details, write: Special Markets, Penguin Group (USA) Inc., 375 Hudson Street, New York, New York 10014.

ACKNOWLEDGMENTS

My deep thanks go to my literary agents, Sheree Bykofsky and Janet Rosen; my excellent editor at Perigee, Meg Leder; Perigee intern Rachel Phaneuf; Perigee copyeditor Candace Levy; my colleague Alison Schoew, who gave me some excellent advice; my friend Justin Gruver, who helped edit the typescript; and my good friend and extraordinary administrative assistant, known for her extraordinary word-processing skills, Robin Hudgins.

This book has been enriched by the hard work of many people. I am grateful.

*The difference between the almost right word
and the right word is really a large matter—it's the difference
between the lightning bug and the lightning.*
—MARK TWAIN

PREFACE

We often only imperfectly understand words that are similar yet distinguishable in meaning. For example, many people know the term *chest of drawers* and know the term *dresser* yet may not realize that a *dresser*, unlike a *chest of drawers*, is expected to support a mirror. Similarly, you may regularly take a *parkway* to work without realizing that a *parkway* is distinguished by being not only broad but also landscaped. Further, *parkways* usually prohibit heavy trucks and other large commercial vehicles.

Still further, many of us may fail to realize that a *frankfurter* won't become a *hot dog* until it is encased in a roll. Unless you're a student of Roman Catholic theology, you may not know that the expression *Immaculate Conception* is not a fancy name for the *Virgin Birth* but is supposed to describe a different event associated with a different person. The dogma of the *Immaculate Conception* refers to a belief that Jesus' mother, Mary, was conceived without *Original Sin*, whereas the *Virgin Birth* is supposed to describe Jesus' birth.

Unfortunately, we aren't always helped by even highly literate authors, such as Arthur Conan Doyle, the creator of Sherlock Holmes. Although Sherlock Holmes often claimed to use *deductive reasoning* in solving his cases, he was usually employing *inductive reasoning*, based not on logical implication (like that used in geometry) but on probabilistic reasoning—inferences that are probably true given the truth of other propositions.

The aim of this book is to clarify hundreds of distinctions that most of us only roughly understand, such as the distinction between a *geek* and a *nerd*, a *dwarf* and a *midget*, and *cement* and *concrete*. To make it into this book, an entry had to distinguish two or more things commonly confused. Many of the things commonly confused are just the sorts of things distinguished by books on English usage (such as *imply* and *infer*). Others are used informally and, often, interchangeably but have technical definitions (*herb* vs. *spice*). Still others are things that culturally literate persons are expected to know, including the distinction mentioned earlier between *inductive* and *deductive reasoning*. Finally, some of the things commonly confused or not fully understood are just plain interesting, especially to trivia lovers, such as the distinction between *gargantuan* and *gigantic*. The former, from the name of a literary character who was a giant (Gargantua) known for his huge appetite, is a word best limited to describing food, drink, appetite, or consumption.

Note that the confused words in this book are listed alphabetically under the first term. Note also that although an entry may function as several parts of speech in different contexts, illustrative sentences use the parts of speech mentioned next to each entry.

A

ABILITY/APTITUDE/TALENT (N.)

Ability is the power, natural or acquired, to perform certain actions or employ certain skills: "He temporarily lost his *ability* to speak."

Aptitude usually implies a natural inclination or disposition, often including a liking for some activity. An *aptitude* might exist without its being developed: "Having an *aptitude* for numbers won't guarantee that one has the discipline and motivation to become a math professor."

Talent often refers to people's natural endowments for artistic or creative work: "Jack's Nicholson's *talent* for acting is impressive."

ABJURE/ADJURE (V.)

To *abjure* is to renounce, repudiate, or give up: "She *abjured* her allegiance to the organization."

To *adjure* is to charge or command solemnly or to entreat or advise earnestly: "The district attorney *adjured* the jurors to consider the evidence impartially before making their decision."

ABRASION/CONTUSION/LACERATION (N.)

Abrasions, *contusions*, and *lacerations* are, respectively, scrapes, bruises, and cuts (or tears): "Bob's *abrasion* on his knee was caused by his fall." "After Wilma struck Fred on his left arm, he had a *contusion*." "Betty's *lacerations* came from falling on broken glass."

ABSOLUTE ZERO/ZERO (N.)

Absolute zero is the term given to the temperature −273.15°C or −459.67°F, at which all molecular motion theoretically ceases: "Scientists cannot cool any substance to *absolute zero*."

Zero on the Celsius scale (32°F) is the temperature at which water freezes: "Minnesota winters bring temperatures far below *zero* Celsius."

ABSTEMIOUS/ABSTINENT (ADJ.)

You are *abstemious* if you are moderate in your habits, especially in consuming food and drink: "The *abstemious* woman drank wine, but never to excess."

Abstinent persons abstain from indulging in various pleasures or yielding to various temptations: "A person who takes vows of chastity is pledging to be sexually *abstinent*, and teetotalers are *abstinent* in their consumption of alcohol."

ABSTRUSE/OBSCURE (ADJ.)

What is *abstruse* is difficult to understand because it requires deep or special knowledge: "Kant's theory of knowledge is too *abstruse* for almost all elementary school students."

What is *obscure* is difficult to understand because it

is unclear: "We had trouble understanding his vague, *obscure* language."

ABUSE/MISUSE (N.)

Abuse constitutes wrong, improper, or bad use, often involving some damage or harm: "Child *abuse* leaves psychological scars, apart from any physical harm it may cause."

Misuse designates incorrect, unorthodox, or unauthorized use that may or may not lead to harm, as when someone misuses a word: "Sometimes people *misuse* the word *infer*, thinking that it means 'imply.' "

Note that verbal *abuse* or *abusive* language involves using language in a way that may damage or harm people.

ACADEMIC/SCHOLASTIC (ADJ.)

To the extent that the two terms are distinguished, *academic* often describes idea-driven disciplines, such as literature and philosophy: "Because the young woman was adroit in thinking independently and writing essays, she particularly liked her most *academic* classes."

Scholastic describes purely factual intellectual pursuits followed in school, such as science, history, and English: "The four students were competitors in the *scholastic* bowl."

ACADIA/ARCADIA (PLACE NAME)

The part of Canada now known as New Brunswick and Nova Scotia was once called *Acadia*: "During the mid-eighteenth century, British soldiers deported residents of *Acadia* who refused to pledge allegiance to the British king." Many of those people who refused to pledge allegiance fled to what is now southern Louisiana (Cajun country).

Arcadia is a region of Greece, whose history goes back to ancient times: "The present-day capital of *Arcadia* is Tripoli, Greece."

ACCIDENT/INCIDENT/MISHAP (N.)

An *accident* is an event that occurs by chance rather than by design. It can be good (a lucky *accident*), bad (a fatal *accident*), or neutral (an *accident* of birth): "The bicycle *accident* occurred at five o'clock."

An *incident* is any event or occurrence, expected or unexpected, good, bad, or neutral: "The argument during the party was an *incident* I missed."

A *mishap* is a minor unfortunate accident: "Accidentally tearing a check one is writing is a *mishap*, but not a disaster."

ACCIDENTAL/INCIDENTAL (ADJ.)

What is *accidental* happens by chance: "We didn't plan our meeting at the restaurant; it was *accidental*."

What is *incidental* occurs as a minor consequence of something more important: "The main advantage of having a small car is that it is inexpensive; an *incidental* advantage is that it is easier to park than a larger car."

ACUITY/ACUMEN (N.)

Acuity is sharpness or keenness of sensory perception or intelligence: "We were impressed by his visual *acuity*, which enabled him to drive his car without wearing glasses."

Acumen implies keen discernment with good judgment: "Bill Gates possesses extraordinary business *acumen*."

ADHERE/COHERE (V.)

To *adhere* is to stick fast—literally, as when masking tape adheres to a surface, or figuratively, as when people adhere to their convictions or religion: "She will never sway from her principles but will always *adhere* to them."

To *cohere* is to stick together (as in mutual support) or to be consistent or harmonious: "The story didn't *cohere* because of contradictory elements."

ADJACENT/ADJOINING/CONTIGUOUS (ADJ.)

Adjacent means "nearby," "joining," or "touching": "The city square was convenient for those living on *adjacent* streets." "We moved the car to the *adjacent* right lane."

Adjoining suggests common boundaries: "She slept in the *adjoining* room."

Contiguous can mean "connected" or "nearby," though it usually implies connection: "Only Alaska and Hawaii exist apart from America's *contiguous* states."

ADVERSARY/ANTAGONIST/OPPONENT (N.)

An *adversary* is a competitor toward whom one needn't feel animosity or hatred: "Business competitors can be *adversaries* without being enemies."

An *antagonist* usually implies sharper opposition than that of an *adversary*, especially in a struggle for supremacy or control; the term also designates the principal foil of the main character in a drama or narrative: "It was evident that either John or his *antagonist* would prevail in the struggle to lead the organization."

Opponent designates one on the opposite side in a contest: "We thought that the hometown team would defeat their current *opponents*."

ADVERSE/AVERSE (ADJ.)

Adverse means "unfavorable" or "hostile," as in *adverse* publicity or *adverse* comments: "Although Paris Hilton often receives *adverse* publicity, millions of people appear to be interested in her."

Averse means "disinclined" or "mildly opposed." *Averse* implies avoidance because of distaste or repugnance. People are said to be *averse* to things, but things are *adverse* to people: "The lazy man was *averse* to hard work."

ADVISEDLY/INTENTIONALLY (ADV.)

An action taken *advisedly* is deliberate and taken with careful consideration. An action taken *intentionally* is done on purpose rather than by accident: "Many citizens strike police officers *intentionally*; few citizens strike police officers *advisedly*."

AFFECT/EFFECT (N./V.)

The word *affect* is usually used as a verb to mean "act on or influence," "move emotionally," or "pretend or imitate": "His sincere apology will *affect* how he will be punished."

As a noun, *affect* means "the conscious, subjective aspect of an emotion" or "the observable manifestation of emotion": "The patient showed little passion, displaying diminished *affect*."

The word *effect* is used principally as a noun, less often as a verb. As a noun, it means "result," "influence," or "the state of being in operation": "The *effects* of a world leader's actions are often unpredictable." "The new program was recently put into *effect*."

As a verb, *effect* means "to bring about": "The presidential candidate promised to *effect* change."

AFFLICT/INFLICT (V.)

To *afflict* is to cause distress to someone: "The villagers were *afflicted* with the plague."

To *inflict* is to impose something unpleasant (such as defeat, punishment, or pain) on someone: "We believed that the punishment *inflicted* on the criminal was appropriate."

Note that, generally speaking, a person is *afflicted with* something, but a thing is *inflicted on* someone.

AFFRONT/EFFRONTERY (N.)

An *affront* is an open insult: "Intentionally arriving late to an important meeting was an *affront* to the host."

Effrontery is brazen boldness, flagrant or flaunted insolence that is rude and presumptuous: "The corrupt politician had the *effrontery* to pose as a protector of morality."

AGGLOMERATE/CONGLOMERATE (N.)

An *agglomerate* is a collection or mass of things that have been tossed or packed together—usually chaotically: "A Prussian spy held that Karl Marx lived in a sloppy London apartment containing a table with an *agglomerate* of items that a secondhand merchant would be embarrassed to carry."

A *conglomerate* is a package or collection of disparate elements that have been thoroughly mixed, such as a corporation that has acquired other companies in related fields (movies, CDs, books): "Many book publishing companies are part of *conglomerates*, with holdings in other areas of media."

ALIBI/EXCUSE (N.)

An *alibi*, strictly speaking, is a plea or fact of having been elsewhere when an offense was committed: "The defendant's *alibi* was that he was out of the country during the commission of the crime."

An *excuse* is an attempt to offer justifying or mitigating reasons for some conduct: "His *excuse* for not completing the assignment was that he was busy helping a friend."

ALLEVIATE/AMELIORATE (V.)

To *alleviate* is to make lighter, easier, or less painful: "The aspirin *alleviated* the pain."

To *ameliorate* is to improve: "Snow plows removed snow from the roads to *ameliorate* road conditions."

ALLOCATE/ALLOT (V.)

To *allocate* is to assign for a specific purpose: "The group *allocated* funds for constructing a new room."

To *allot* is to assign as a share or portion: "Each debater was *allotted* five minutes for summary."

ALLOY/AMALGAM (N.)

An *alloy* literally designates a substance composed of two or more metals intimately mixed, as in brass, and figuratively refers to an admixture that lessens value or detracts from quality: "Brass is an *alloy* of copper and zinc." "The politician had his *alloy* of public-spiritedness and selfishness."

An *amalgam*, most literally, is an *alloy* made by adding mercury to a metal; the term has been especially used in dental restoration. Figuratively, *amalgam* often implies a combination of different elements, emphasizing the complexity of the mixtures: "Our judgment of literary figures is often an *amalgam* of our judgments of their works and of the authors themselves."

ALL TOGETHER/ALTOGETHER (ADV.)

All together means "in a group": "The cooks were *all together* in the kitchen."

Altogether means "wholly," "entirely," or "completely": "The two situations were different and *altogether* distinct."

ALLUSIVE/ELUSIVE (ADJ.)

Allusive means "referring indirectly" or "hinting": "The man didn't accuse her directly but *allusively*."

What is *elusive* is difficult to discover, catch, recall, or pin down: "The police had trouble finding the *elusive* fugitive."

ALUMNUS (ALUMNI)/ALUMNA (ALUMNAE) (N.)

An *alumnus* is a male graduate of a school; an *alumna* is a female graduate of a school: "John was an *alumnus* of Harvard, and Jane was an *alumna* of Yale."

The plural of *alumnus* is *alumni*, as many people know, and the plural of *alumna* is *alumnae*, as fewer people know.

AMBIGUOUS/AMBIVALENT/EQUIVOCAL/ VAGUE (ADJ.)

Something *ambiguous* has more than one meaning. Anything said, written, or done can be *ambiguous*: "His *ambiguous* statement was susceptible to two different interpretations."

Ambivalent means "having conflicting feelings": "We were *ambivalent* about the new job because it meant a larger salary but required moving to a less attractive city."

Equivocal often describes what is purposely ambiguous, admitting of a false interpretation designed to deceive or evade: "Advertisements often contain *equivocal* language, as when a car is said to get 'up to' thirty miles in the city, when that figure is arrived at only under optimal conditions and may not be the typical mileage."

What is *vague* is indefinite or indeterminate in meaning or scope: "The word *bald* (as applied to someone's head) is *vague* because it can properly be used while people still have some hair, and there is no exact and determinate point in the process of depilation at which the person losing hair must first be said to be bald."

AMBROSIA/NECTAR (N.)

In classical mythology, *ambrosia* was the food of the gods; *nectar*, the drink of the gods: "Although the drinks at the party were good enough to be called *nectar*, the food fell short of *ambrosia*."

AMEND/EMEND (V.)

To *amend* is to make changes that improve the quality of something, whatever it may be: "It is hard to *amend* the Constitution, but easier than *amending* human nature."

To *emend* is to free from error or defect, especially false or inaccurate oral or written statements: "We had to *emend* the financial report."

AMIABLE/AMICABLE (ADJ.)

Amiable means "friendly," "pleasing," or "easy to like": "*Amiable* people are easy to befriend."

Amicable usually refers to relationships, agreements, divorces, and settlements and means "characterized by friendliness and goodwill" or "peaceable": "Given the general unpleasantness of divorce, my friend's divorce was fairly *amicable*."

AMOK (AMUCK) (ADV.)/BERSERK (ADJ.)

To run *amok* is literally and originally meant to commit indiscriminate murder, though it often means "to act in an undisciplined, uncontrolled, or faulty manner." In the latter sense, even computers can run *amok*. The word comes from a Malay word referring to men who went out in the street and killed anyone they met: "Mass killers who go to shopping malls and proceed to kill people indiscriminately run *amok*."

To go *berserk* is to behave crazily and violently or to act with reckless defiance. *Berserk* can also describe someone who has completely lost composure and emotional self-control, as when someone becomes *ber-*

serk with grief. The word *berserk* comes from the Old Norse word *berserkr* ("a wild warrior or champion"). Those Norse warriors became frenzied in battle, howling like animals, foaming at the mouth, and even biting the edges of their iron shields: "When the man was fired, he went *berserk*, throwing chairs out of the window."

AMORAL/IMMORAL/NONMORAL (ADJ.)

Amoral can mean "nonmoral" or "outside the bounds of that to which moral distinctions apply": "Rocks, apart from their use by people, are *amoral* or *nonmoral*." We often use *amoral* to mean "without moral sensibility," as in describing sociopaths, who are without normal moral feeling: "The serial killer was without any conscience—totally *amoral*."

Immoral means "contrary to conscience or moral law": "Seriously harming others simply for one's social advancement is *immoral*."

Nonmoral describes things not subject to moral evaluation: "The sand at the bottom of an ocean, unlike a person's conduct, is *nonmoral*."

AMOUNT/NUMBER (N.)

An *amount* is a quantity reckoned in mass or bulk: "We couldn't believe the *amount* of traffic on the road."

A *number* is a quantity reckoned in quantifiable units: "A large *number* of scholars attended the conference."

AMUSE/BEMUSE (V.)

Amuse means "to entertain or to provide with pleasure," whereas *bemuse* means "to confuse or bewilder": "The illogical testimony from the prosecutor's witness *amused* the defense counsel but *bemused* the jurors."

ANALOGOUS/HOMOLOGOUS (ADJ.)

Analogous features of organisms resemble one another in function but have completely different origins: "The wings of birds and insects have *analogous* functions."

Homologous features of organisms were originally the same in evolutionary development but have adapted differently: "The scales of fish and the wings of birds are *homologous*."

ANNALS/CHRONICLES (N.)

Annals, strictly speaking, are yearly records of events or achievements (from the Latin root *annus* for "year"): "In the *annals* of San Francisco for 1967, one would expect to see the expression 'the summer of love.' "

Chronicles (from the Greek root *chrono-* for "time") are records of any substantial historical event, whether a war or a reign: "The Bible contains *chronicles* of events important to ancient Israel."

ANTICIPATE/EXPECT (V.)

In careful usage, *anticipate* implies foreseeing and dealing with in advance: "His speech showed that he had *anticipated* objections."

Expect can describe considering something probable or certain or looking forward to some event: "We *expect* her to arrive at any moment."

ANTIPERSPIRANT/DEODORANT (N.)

An *antiperspirant* reduces sweat; a *deodorant* destroys or masks unpleasant odors: "Whereas *deodorants* act by retarding the growth of bacteria, *antiperspirants* retard the growth of bacteria *and* suppress perspiration."

ANXIOUS/EAGER (ADJ.)

In careful usage, *anxious* connects with anxiety, a feeling of worry or apprehension: "When people focus on all that may go wrong, they tend to feel *anxious*."

Eager describes a strong and urgent interest, desire, or enthusiasm: "We were *eager* to collect our prize."

APEX/EPITOME (N.)

An *apex* is the highest or uppermost point—that is, the summit or peak (the *apex* of the mountain). The word can also designate a culminating point (the *apex* of his career): "Few persons have reached the *apex* of Mount Everest."

Epitome is a brief summary (as of a written work) or a typical representation or ideal expression: "To many people, a Boy Scout who has earned the rank of Eagle Scout is the *epitome* of wholesomeness."

APHORISM/APOTHEGM/MAXIM/ PROVERB/SAW (N.)

An *aphorism* is a pithy instructive saying embodying a general truth discovered and confirmed by experience: "Some of the earliest and most widely celebrated *aphorisms* are those of Hippocrates, who said, for example, that when two illnesses arrive at the same time, the stronger silences the weaker." "Benjamin

Franklin expressed many *aphorisms* in his *Poor Richard's Almanack*."

An *apothegm* is a sharply pointed (possibly cynical) *aphorism*: "Dr. Samuel Johnson's remark that patriotism is the last refuge of scoundrels qualifies as an *apothegm*."

A *maxim* can embody a general truth, but it typically advises or recommends a course of action, possibly moralistically: " 'Develop good habits, and let them be your master' was his *maxim*."

A *proverb* embodies practical wisdom, usually in homely and vividly concrete phrases: " 'A mouse in time may bite in two a cable' is a *proverb* about perseverance."

A *saw* is an often repeated and usually traditional saying: "The man liked to pass on to his children wise *saws* that he had absorbed from his teachers."

APOLOGIA/APOLOGY (N.)

An *apologia* is a formally expressed (often in writing) defense or vindication of one's belief, conduct, or cause: "The Unabomber's manifesto contained an *apologia* in which he defended his letter bombs by the need to alert people to the dangers of runaway technology."

Apology, though sometimes an *apologia*, is more usually an expression of guilt and regret for wrong or otherwise inappropriate conduct: "We accepted her *apology* for her mistake."

APT/LIABLE/LIKELY (ADJ.)

In the most careful usage, *apt* suggests fitness or tendency: "She is *apt* at creative writing." "He is *apt* to [inclined to] support any candidate who believes in reducing the size of government."

Note that the opposite of *apt* is usually *inept*, though *inapt* is a word.

Liable means either "being exposed to something unwanted, disadvantageous, or burdensome" or "responsible or answerable": "She'll be *liable* to a fine if she litters."

Something *likely* is expected or probable: "She is the most *likely* candidate for the position."

ARBITRATOR/MEDIATOR (N.)

An *arbitrator* is charged with definitely settling, through binding procedures, differences between two parties: "The *arbitrator's* decision was completely in favor of one of the parties."

A *mediator* serves as an intermediary to help other parties reconcile their differences: "The *mediator* helped us resolve our differences."

ARCHAIC/OBSOLETE (ADJ.)

An old term with limited use (as in law, poetry, or ceremonies) is *archaic*: "The expressions *malice aforethought* (in law), *saith* (in biblical or ecclesiastical language), and *methinks* (in poetry or historical fiction) are examples of *archaic* language."

Obsolete words no longer have any use, except perhaps in crossword puzzles or as examples of *obsolete* language: "*Argentum* can be considered an *obsolete* word for silver."

ARGOT/DIALECT/JARGON/LINGO (N.)

Argot is a specialized vocabulary or a set of idioms used by a particular group, designed to be used by insiders only: "People who regularly use or sell illegal drugs are expected to know the appropriate *argot* of illegal drugs, including the use of the word *acid* to designate LSD."

A *dialect* is a language distinguishable from other varieties of the same language by such features as grammar, vocabulary, or pronunciation and is characteristic of a specific group of language users. *Dialects* usually evolve among language users who are set apart geographically: "Different English dialects contain different pronunciations of words, such as *aunt, caramel, creek,* and *pajamas.*"

Jargon applies especially to the language or vocabulary of a particular trade, profession, or organization, such as the technical words used by physicians, lawyers, photographers, and police officers. The word *jargon* comes from a Middle English word meaning "unintelligible speech or gibberish": "Physicians need to use less medical *jargon* around their patients and translate the medical terms into ordinary language."

Lingo is a pejorative term to describe language the user of the term doesn't easily or readily understand: "The young man was unfamiliar with the *lingo* of high finance."

ARITHMETIC/MATHEMATICS (N.)

Arithmetic is the foundational branch of mathematics, dealing with addition, subtraction, multiplication, division, and the laws applying to calculations: "To make change from a dollar, all one needs is *arithmetic*."

Mathematics is the study of the relationships among numbers, shapes, and quantities using signs, symbols, and proofs, and includes arithmetic, algebra, geometry, trigonometry, and calculus: "In the subbranch of the branch of *mathematics* known as algebra, there is elementary algebra, which includes symbols as placeholders to denote constants and variables."

ARMORY/ARSENAL (N.)

Either word can designate a collection of or storehouse for arms and other military equipment. *Armory*, in military language, often describes a storehouse on a military base, and *arsenal* describes the weapons collectively: "We were impressed by the *arsenal* held in the *armory*."

AROUSE/ROUSE (V.)

To *arouse* is to wake people from sleep or to stimulate them or stir them up: "Her remarks *aroused* debate."

Rouse usually applies to stirring into (physical) action: "The fatalities at the intersection *roused* the authorities to install a traffic light."

Rouse suggests previous inactivity, whereas *arouse* suggests stimulating something lying dormant. Sexual desires are usually *aroused*.

ARRANT/ERRANT (ADJ.)

Something *arrant* possesses an undesirable attribute completely; it means "outstandingly bad in some respect": "An *arrant* liar shouldn't be trusted."

Errant means "roving" or "wandering" (knight-*errant*): "The *errant* reporter was always traveling somewhere."

ARTIST/ARTISTE (N.)

An *artist* practices some fine art (such as painting) or is a public performer, as of music or drama: "Salvador Dalí was an imaginative surrealist *artist*."

An *artiste*, often considered a pretentious-sounding term, is a skilled public performer, especially a musical or theatrical entertainer: "The singer Madonna has been an *artiste* with extraordinary business acumen."

ASSAIL/ASSAULT (V.)

Both words can mean "to attack," though *assail* is more likely to be used figuratively and abstractly: "When the politician was *assailed* with questions about changes in her views, she was *assailed* with doubts about her ability to win the election."

To *assault* can be to execute a violent attack, as when soldiers *assault* an enemy. Alternatively, to *assault* (in law) can be to threaten harm without proper cause, as when someone menacingly waves a cane at someone with whom he has an argument: "The man *assaulted* the boy by placing a knife next to the boy's neck."

ASSAULT/BATTERY (N.)

Assault is a threat or an attempt to cause physical harm to someone else, whether successful or unsuccessful: "When the man waved a knife near the other man's head, he was arrested and charged with *assault*."

Battery is fulfilling the threat or attempting to cause

physical harm and using force against another person, with one's bare hands, a weapon, or a projectile (such as a rock or a glass): "When the student hit the teacher with a ruler, he was arrested and charged with *battery.*"

ASSENT/CONSENT (N.)

Both *assent* and *consent* indicate agreement, though *assent* primarily implies the understanding of opinions or propositions: "We expressed our *assent* to the proposition that all citizens deserve equal treatment under law."

Consent involves the will or the feelings, and implies compliance with what is desired or requested: "Gaining parental *consent* to marry Debbie will be challenging."

ASSOCIATION/FEDERATION/LEAGUE (N.)

An *association* (or society) is a group of people banded together to advance shared interests: "The NAACP is an *association* to advance and protect the interest of ethnic minorities."

A *federation* is a union formed by merging groups, each aiming at the common good while retaining a large measure of autonomy: "The American Federation of Labor was one of the first *federations* of labor unions in the United States."

A *league* is an alliance of associations banded together to enable them to pursue common interests more effectively: "The National Hockey *League* consists of more than two dozen teams that have a common interest in North American professional hockey."

ASSURE/ENSURE/INSURE (V.)

To *assure* is to convince, state earnestly, guarantee, or make a person or thing sure: "I was *assured* that everything was safe."

To *ensure* is to make a thing certain: "Can you *ensure* that the car will have safe brakes?"

To *insure* is to guarantee against loss, as through paying insurance: "We'll need to *insure* the new car against damages."

ATOLL/ISLAND (N.)

An *atoll* is a coral reef appearing above the sea as a low ring-shaped coral *island* or as a chain of closely spaced coral islets around a shallow lagoon. In short, an *atoll* is an *island* shaped like a ring and nearly or completely encircling a lagoon: "An *atoll* may be attractive to look at, but many of them aren't big enough for thriving tourist centers."

An *island* is a piece of land, other than a continent, surrounded by water: "Although Australia is surrounded by water, most people don't consider it an *island* but rather a continent."

ATTIC/GARRET/LOFT (N.)

An *attic* or *loft* is the space between the ceiling of the top floor and the roof. A *loft* can also designate the upper space of a barn (barn *loft*) or a church (organ or choir *loft*).

A *garret* is a room in an attic (or *loft*): "We had our meeting in the *garret* of my friend's *attic* [or *loft*]."

AUGMENT/SUPPLEMENT (V.)

You *augment* by adding more of the same thing: "I *augmented* my income by working more hours."

You *supplement* something by making up for a deficiency, as when you complete something or add a finishing touch: "He took vitamins to *supplement* his dietary deficiencies."

AUGURY/AUSPICE (N.)

Both *augury* and *auspice* are omens or portents, indicating the future, but an *auspice* is usually favorable: "Hitler's rise to power was an *augury* of future conflict." "We were hoping that the falling rate of violent crime in town was an *auspice* of things to come."

AUSPICIOUS/PROPITIOUS (ADJ.)

Something that is *auspicious* indicates good fortune or future success: "Selling ten thousand copies of this book in two weeks was an *auspicious* event."

Propitious can forecast good future, but it describes what is favorable now and what is likely to continue to be favorable. In short, *propitious* can mean "opportune" or "advantageous": "This is a *propitious* time for the merger."

AUTHORITARIAN/AUTHORITATIVE (ADJ.)

Authoritarian describes dictatorial power, whereas *authoritative* describes expert or definitive information: "The man's *authoritarian* manner was his compensation for lacking *authoritative* knowledge."

AUTOMATION/MECHANIZATION (N.)

Automation involves using an apparatus, process, or system that takes the place of human observation, effort, and decision: "The *automation* provided by an electronic security system made a human security guard unnecessary."

Mechanization occurs when people use machines to do their jobs: "Operating a drill press at work involves *mechanization*."

AVENGE/REVENGE (V.)

Both *avenge* and *revenge* involve punishing a person who has wronged someone. *Avenge*, however, suggests either punishing a person on behalf of someone who was wronged or serving the ends of justice: "The district attorney was determined to *avenge* the innocent woman's death."

Revenge more often applies to vindicating oneself and usually suggests an evening up of scores more than an achievement of justice, often connoting spite or vindictive retaliation: "Because each tribe wanted to *revenge* previous acts of retaliation, the two tribes were constantly fighting."

AVERT/AVOID (V.)

To *avert* is to turn away (as one's eyes) or to prevent or ward off: "We need to meet with our enemies if we are to *avert* war."

To *avoid* is to escape some danger: "We weren't able to prevent the accident, but we were able to *avoid* being involved in it."

AWHILE (ADV.)/A WHILE (ART. AND N.)

Awhile is an adverb describing a short time: "Although you have to leave soon, you can still chat *awhile*."

A while consists of two words, an article and a noun, and means "a time": "Please stay for *a while*."

AX/HATCHET/TOMAHAWK (N.)

An *ax* is a double-handed cutting tool with an iron or steel head blade on one side and a usually flat edge on the other: "We used the *ax* for felling trees and chopping and splitting wood."

A *hatchet* is a single-handed, short-handled *ax* used to cut and split wood: "The *hatchet* had a hammer head."

A *tomahawk* is a light *ax*, capable of being swung with one hand and used as a missile, hand weapon, or tool, especially by North American Indians: "The early *tomahawk* had a stone head."

B

BALCONY/DECK/PATIO/PORCH/TERRACE/ VERANDA (N.)

A *balcony* is usually a small, flat projection from the side of a building, with a stone or metal railing and enough room for perhaps a table and a few chairs. *Balconies* may be attached to private houses or apartments: "We like to drink coffee on the *balcony*."

In the United States, a *deck* is a fairly large *balcony* of a house, usually built of wood and supported by columns fixed into the ground. Originating in summerhouses and beach houses, *decks* have become popular in private homes and are often added as improvements: "We had a cookout to enjoy our new *deck*."

A *patio* area is a paved area adjoining a house, used for lounging and entertaining: "We had a small cookout on the *patio*."

A *porch* and a *veranda* are the same object in America and Canada—namely, a roofed gallery along an exterior wall of a house, enclosed by a railing and sometimes screening to keep away insects: "During the fall we like to sit on the *porch* to talk and enjoy the sights and sounds of nature."

A *terrace* is a colonnaded *porch* or promenade,

sometimes a *balcony* or *deck*, and a flat paved or planted area adjoining a building, often surrounded by a balustrade: "The formal English *terrace* was surrounded by a balustrade."

BALEFUL/BANEFUL (N.)

Baleful, from the archaic noun *bale* ("evil," "misery"), refers to what threatens inevitable misery, suffering, or destruction, often imputing perniciousness or hellishness to the thing so described. What is *baleful* can work its evil openly or occultly: "Hitler's rise to power meant that he would be able to implement his *baleful* plans."

What is *baneful*, from words meaning "wound," "death," or "destruction," may describe anything malevolent or malignant that is likely to poison, kill, or destroy: "We are all too familiar with the *baneful* effects of totalitarianism."

BALUSTER/BANISTER (N.)

Balusters are short, vertical posts, sometimes elaborately shaped or carved, supporting *banisters*, which are handrails of staircases: "It is *banisters*, not *balusters*, down which children slide."

BANISH/DEPORT/EXILE/EXPATRIATE (V.)

To *banish* people is to expel them from a country, usually forcing them to live where they don't want to live: "The American protagonist Philip Nolan, in the short story 'The Man Without a Country,' was *banished* to American warships for being an accomplice to treason and cursing the United States."

To *deport* people implies forcibly removing aliens who have illegally entered or whose presence is judged inimical to the public welfare: "The politician asserted that it would be impossible to find and *deport* every illegal alien in the United States."

Exiling people often involves compulsory removal or an enforced absence, though people can *exile* themselves: "Some writers *exile* themselves for political reasons."

People *expatriate* when they leave their native country to live elsewhere or renounce their allegiance to their native country. Usually *expatriate* describes self-removal, though it can describe taking away people's citizenship or sending them away from their native countries as punishment: "Bobby Fischer, the former world chess champion who died in January 2008, had *expatriated*, living and dying in Iceland."

BASEMENT/CELLAR (N.)

A *basement* is a story immediately below the main floor and wholly or partly underground: "We kept the exercise equipment in the *basement*."

A *cellar* is a room or group of rooms in the basement commonly used for storing things, such as food, wine, and wood: "We stored the wine in our *cellar*."

BAY/COVE/GULF (N.)

A *bay* is an arm of a sea or an ocean, forming an indentation in the shoreline that is no more than several miles wide at its mouth: "Lying off the Atlantic Ocean, the Chesapeake *Bay* is surrounded by Maryland and Virginia."

A *cove* is a small bay: "The map's irregular shoreline is broken by several *coves*."

A *gulf* is a large section of a sea or an ocean enclosed

on three sides by land, forming a body of water with its own currents and weather systems: "In Florida, we enjoyed boating in the *gulf*."

BAYOU/BOG/MARSH/SWAMP (N.)

A *bayou* is any stagnant body of water with sparse vegetation.

A *bog* is wet and spongy ground, covered not with trees but with decayed vegetable matter, especially moss. *Bogs* usually develop from ponds or lakes with poor drainage.

A *marsh* is an open, airy place, usually with lush grass and cattails growing in it and covered with water.

A *swamp* is wet, spongy land where trees, such as the bald cypress, grow: "We know that we were in a *bayou* and not a *bog*, *marsh*, or *swamp* because we saw stagnant water and very little vegetation."

BELLICOSE/BELLIGERENT (ADJ.)

Bellicose usually applies to a state of mind or temper, suggesting a readiness to fight or to stir up a fight: "The drunkard was in a *bellicose* mood, eager to create a confrontation."

Belligerent often applies to actual engagement in hostilities, as in "*belligerent* nations." *Belligerent* can also describe tone, speech, or gestures that reveal hostility or combativeness: "The student's reply betrayed a *belligerent* attitude toward authority.

BENEFICENT/BENEVOLENT/BENIGN (ADJ.)

Beneficent, applying to persons and things, means "doing or effecting good": "We praised her for her *beneficent* acts."

Benevolent, applying primarily to persons, means "kindly in feelings and charitable": "A *benevolent* person wants to promote people's happiness because of a kind heart."

Benign, when describing people rather than nonmalignant tumors, emphasizes mildness and mercifulness. Further, *benign* often carries the idea of graciousness, so that it often applies to the actions, utterances, or policies of superiors rather than equals: "He was sensitive to the effects of his decisions on peasants and was a *benign* king."

BESIDE (PREP.)/BESIDES (PREP., ADV., ADJ.)

Beside functions as a preposition meaning "by the side of," "in comparison with," "on a par with," or "not relevant to": "I stood *beside* her."

Besides can function as a preposition meaning "except" or "in addition to." It can also function as an adverb meaning "also" or "furthermore" or as an adjective meaning "else": "No one *besides* you will be dressed in formal wear."

BIANNUAL/BIENNIAL (ADJ.)

A *biannual* event occurs twice a year, whereas a *biennial* event occurs every two years: "The member of the House of Representatives scheduled his upcoming *biannual* dental appointment on the same day as his *biennial* election."

BIAS/PREJUDICE (N.)

A *bias* is an imbalance or a distortion in judgment, predictably pulling someone in a direction because of the person's fixed ideas: "Even though the business owner knew she was hiring someone less competent than the person she rejected, she hired him because of a *bias* in favor of her school's alumni."

Prejudice applies to a judgment made before evidence has been properly examined and typically based on an unfavorable preconception marked by suspicion or hostility: "The juror's racial *prejudice* made it difficult for her to assess the evidence impartially."

The idea, then, of unreasonably prejudging (often negatively) is essential to *prejudice* but not to *bias*.

BISECT/DISSECT (V.)

To *bisect* is to divide something into two usually equal parts: "The diameter of a circle *bisects* it."

To *dissect* is to cut apart piece by piece: "We had to *dissect* a frog in biology class."

BIT PART/CAMEO/EXTRA/WALK-ON (N.)

A *bit part* is a small role of a supporting actor, calling for at least one line of dialogue and often several lines: "Because he had a *bit part*, he was listed in the credits."

A *cameo* (or *cameo* appearance) is a brief appearance of a famous person (often not an actor) in a movie, play, or TV show. *Cameos* are small, and most of them are nonspeaking: "Alfred Hitchcock made *cameos* in more than thirty of his movies."

An *extra* is an anonymous person appearing in a nonspeaking role, usually in the background as a pedestrian, a patron of a restaurant, or a person sitting on a bench: "Some movies have literally dozens, even hundreds, of *extras*."

A *walk-on* is marginally more important than an *extra* because a *walk-on* is clearly seen, usually performing some easily identifiable action, such as taking an order at a restaurant or writing someone a parking ticket: "Some famous actors began their careers as *extras* or *walk-ons*."

BLATANT/FLAGRANT (ADJ.)

Something *blatant* is vulgar, offensively noisy, crassly displayed, or brazenly indifferent to others' feelings: "The elderly couple was shocked at the students' *blatant* profanity."

Something *flagrant* is an error, offense, or evil that is so conspicuously or outstandingly bad as to be incapable of avoiding notice or condemnation: "President Nixon's cover-up of the Watergate burglary involved a *flagrant* violation of power."

BLUSH/FLUSH (V.)

To *blush* is to become suddenly red in the face because of embarrassment, shame, or confusion: "Some people *blush* when a discussion turns to sex."

Flush can be a synonym of *blush*, but it usually describes the rapid and sudden flow of anything: "The tide began to *flush* through the inlet."

BOAST/BRAG (V.)

To *boast* is to draw attention to and express pride about one's deeds or attributes, or those of others (such as family or connections) to whom one is closely related. To *boast* may but needn't involve conceit, exaggeration, or ostentation: "The governor took time to *boast* about the accomplishments of her administration."

To *brag*, however, tends to imply conceit and exaggeration, often glorying in one's superior attributes or abilities: "The drunken men *bragged* about the extraordinarily large fish they had caught."

BOUGH/BRANCH (N.)

Both *bough* and *branch* designate a limb of tree, but a *bough* is a main *branch*, whereas a *branch* can be any limb: "The *bough* had many *branches*."

BOULEVARD/LANE/ROAD/STREET (N.)

In the United States, a *boulevard* is a wide and long street, especially one with trees on both sides, down the middle, or both: "The *boulevard* was known for its attractive landscaping and impressive width."

A *lane* is a narrow path, road, or street, often in older town areas or in the countryside and often enclosed by walls or hedges: "It can be difficult to find enough room to park in a *lane*."

A *road* is an open way on which vehicles or people can travel: "When driving, one should always keep one's eye on the *road*."

A *street* is a *road*, especially in an urban environment, usually lined with buildings and often with sidewalks: "The woman doesn't like strangers' parking in front of her home, even though they are parking on a public *street*."

BRANDY/COGNAC (N.)

Brandy is a spirit distilled from wine or sometimes fruit juice (as plum or cherry *brandy*).

Cognac properly designates French *brandy*, usually

regarded as the finest of all *brandies*, distilled from the wine of the region around Cognac, a town in western France: "The wine expert chided us for calling our *brandy 'cognac'* because it was not produced in France at all, much less Cognac, France."

BRASS/BRONZE (N.)

Brass is an alloy of copper and zinc (sometimes with small amounts of other elements): "The door knocker was made of *brass*."

Bronze is an alloy of copper and tin (sometimes with small amounts of other elements): "The tools made of *bronze* were ancient."

BRAVADO/BRAVERY/BRAVURA (N.)

Bravado is a blustering display of defiance or pretended bravery: "The boy's ostentatious refusal to go to bed was not courage but mere *bravado*."

Bravery is courage: "The soldier received a medal for the *bravery* he displayed on the battlefield."

Bravura can refer to any showy display, but it has special application to music, where it describes brilliant technique or style, or a piece of music emphasizing a performer's virtuosity: "We were enormously impressed by the *bravura* displayed by pianist Glenn Gould."

BRING/FETCH/TAKE (V.)

Bring implies carrying, leading, or transporting from a distance to the place where the speaker or agent is or will be: "The teacher asked the student to *bring* his homework to her."

Fetch implies going to a place where something is to

be found, getting it, and transporting it to the starting point: "I arose from my seat to *fetch* a pen from another student."

Take implies carrying, leading, or conducting to a place away from where the speaker or agent is or will be: "The teacher asked me to *take* a note home to my parents and to have them sign it."

BROOK/CREEK/STREAM (N.)

A *brook* is a current of water normally smaller than a *creek* or *stream*. *Brooks* are often shallow or intermittent tributaries of rivers. They can form from water that seeps up from the ground or from substantial rainfall: "The *brook* was small enough for the girl to step over."

A *creek* is a current of water that is normally smaller than a *stream* but larger than a *brook* and is often a tributary of a river: "We were at the point where the *creek* flows into the river."

A *stream* is a body of flowing freshwater usually smaller than a river, though sometimes the term applies to a narrow and shallow river. *Streams* can be intermittent (running only part of the year) or perennial (running year-round). They can also be gaining (taking in water from underground pockets) or losing (leaking water into underground pockets): "The *stream* was shallow enough for us to wade through."

BRUTAL/BRUTISH (ADJ.)

Brutal is applied almost exclusively to human beings or their acts or character, implying a lack of humane feeling and describing animalistic behavior. The word emphasizes gross inhumanity and cruelty: "The serial killer was *brutal* in his torture."

Brutish, also usually applied to human beings and their acts, normally doesn't stress cruelty and inhumanity but rather extreme stupidity, lack of control over appetite, and government by instinct rather than reason: "The serial killer wasn't necessarily *brutish*, because he displayed high intelligence and self-control."

BUG/INSECT (N.)

Bugs are wingless or four-winged *insects* of the order Hemiptera ("half-winged"), characterized by their sucking mouthparts originating from the tips of their heads. Their forewings are also differentiated with a thickened base and membranous tip. *Bugs* lack teeth and don't chew. Most *bugs* suck plant material (especially sap), but some, such as bed*bugs*, suck animal blood: "At the zoo, we saw land *bugs*, including aphids, stink*bugs*, and lice."

Insects are invertebrates in the class Insecta, each of whose members has three body parts (head, thorax, and abdomen), six jointed legs, two antennae to sense the world around it, and an exoskeleton (external skeleton): "Caterpillars and butterflies are *insects*."

BULL/CATTLE/COW/OX/STEER (N.)

Bulls are uncastrated male *cattle*. *Cows* are female *cattle*, and *steers* are castrated male *cattle*: "The *bull* and the *cow* produced a healthy calf."

Steers and *oxen* are the same animal, though the former term usually applies to animals raised for beef, and the latter usually applies to draft animals: "We used the *steers* for beef and used the *oxen* for carrying things."

BUM/HOBO/TRAMP (N.)

A *bum* sponges off others and avoids work: "The *bum* lived with his sister and refused to get a job."

The term *hobo* has been used in the past to describe a person who liked being transient, often moving from place to place but taking temporary jobs: "The *hobo* hopped the train for a ride."

A *tramp*, in the current context, can apply to someone without an established residence, wandering idly from place to place without lawful or visible means of support: "*Tramps* have been criticized for lacking a work ethic and strong ties to communities."

BUNION/CORN (N.)

A *bunion* is an enlargement of the first joint of the big toe because of an inflammation and swelling of the bursa (a sac at the joint) at the base of the big toe: "Because of his *bunion*, his big toe pointed to the side."

A *corn* is a hard thickening of the skin (especially on the top or sides of the toes) caused by friction or compression: "She developed *corns* from her ill-fitting shoes."

BURGLARY/ROBBERY (N.)

Burglary is the theft of property without the owner's awareness of the crime while the theft is occurring. "The *burglary* happened when they were on vacation."

Robbery is the theft of property by force and fear,

so that it necessarily involves confrontation between criminals and victims: "The bank clerk was fearful of returning to work after witnessing the *robbery*."

BUSH/SHRUB (N.)

A *bush* is a low *shrub* with many branches: "The *bush* by the garage was our most densely branched plant."

A *shrub* is a woody plant smaller than a tree: "In the Arctic, where trees don't thrive, *shrubs* are a valuable source of food and wood."

BY HEART/BY ROTE (ADV.)

If you know something *by heart*, you know it perfectly, even if you haven't learned it in any formal setting: "The woman knew the song *by heart*, not because she had studied it but because she had heard it numerous times."

If you learned something *by rote*, you learned it deliberately and mechanically by constantly repeating or rehearsing it: "The pupil learned the multiplication tables *by rote*."

C

CADAVER/CARCASS/CORPSE/REMAINS (N.)

A *cadaver* is a dead body intended for dissection: "Medical students dissect *cadavers*."

A *carcass* is a term for a slaughtered animal from which the inedible sections have been removed: "The birds were gnawing on the *carcass* of the dead animal."

A *corpse* is a dead human body, especially one that has not been embalmed: "The *corpse* was removed from the crime scene."

The term *remains* applies to an embalmed body, a body whose major sections have been removed in dissection, or a body much of whose soft tissue has fallen away over time: "At the funeral home, we viewed the *remains*."

CALAMITY/CATACLYSM/CATASTROPHE (N.)

A *calamity* is a grievous misfortune involving either great or far-reaching personal or public loss, or profound (and widespread) distress: "The assassination of President John F. Kennedy was a *calamity* that distressed millions of people."

A *cataclysm* is an event or situation overwhelming the old order, or a violent social or political upheaval: "The storming of the Bastille marked the beginning of the *cataclysm* known as the French Revolution."

A *catastrophe* is an event that has a disastrous conclusion: "A serious rupture in the levy would lead to a *catastrophe* for people living in low-lying areas."

CAN/MAY (AUX. V.)

Can is a verb used to indicate physical or mental ability: "The young boy *can* count to fifty."

May, when distinguished from *can*, means "to be allowed or permitted to": "*May* I go to the bathroom, please?"

CAPE/CLOAK (N.)

A *cape* is a sleeveless garment fastened around the neck and falling from the shoulders: "*Capes* worn by men are typically black and sometimes lined with silk (often red)."

A *cloak* is also sleeveless and fastened around the neck but is somewhat fuller than a *cape* and worn over clothing, much as an overcoat is worn and often for the same reason—to protect the wearer against cold or inclement weather. *Cloaks*, which have buttons in front to secure them, are usually made of heavier material and have hoods (cowls): "She bought a new *cloak* when the temperature dropped."

CAPE/ISTHMUS/PENINSULA (N.)

A *cape* is a point of land jutting out into water, especially one important for navigation: "The *Cape* of Good Hope is near the southern tip of Africa, but it isn't the southernmost point."

An *isthmus* is a narrow strip of land bordered on two sides by water and connecting two larger bodies of land: "An excellent example of an *isthmus* is Panama, which connects the north and south part of America."

A *peninsula* is a piece of land that is bordered on three sides by water: "Florida, the land mass encompassing North and South Korea, and the Indian subcontinent are all *peninsulas*."

CARCINOMA/MELANOMA/SARCOMA (N.)

A *carcinoma* is any malignant cancer arising from epithelial cells, which line the cavities and surfaces of structures throughout the body and make up many glands, such as the exocrine and endocrine glands. *Carcinomas* often originate in the epithelial tissue of the breast, colon, and pancreas: "An analysis of his pancreas revealed *carcinoma*."

A *melanoma* is a malignant tumor beginning in the melanocytes (the epidermal cells producing melanin) of normal skin or moles and spreading rapidly: "The analysis of the mole on the man's neck revealed *melanoma*."

A *sarcoma* is a cancer of the connective or supportive tissue (bone, cartilage, fat, muscle, blood vessels) and soft tissue: "Analysis of the woman's femur revealed Ewing's *sarcoma*."

CAREER/LIVELIHOOD/OCCUPATION/ PROFESSION/TRADE/VOCATION (N.)

A *career* is both the job or occupation regarded as a long-term or lifelong activity, and someone's progress in a chosen profession or during the person's working life:

"Because she was good at working with numbers and loved mathematics, we suggested a *career* in engineering."

Livelihood applies to the means by which one earns money, which can vary from day to day: "The town derived its *livelihood* from farming."

Occupation suggests a steady or principal line of work or business: "It is often difficult for people to move from nontechnical *occupations* to more technical ones."

Profession implies an occupation requiring extensive training or education: "Most persons in the legal *profession* need to be able to read carefully, attending to nuances in meaning."

Trade can describe a skilled occupation often requiring manual labor or one involving limited training in a particular area: "Plumbing is a *trade* that in the United States typically pays well."

A *vocation* is a person's employment or main occupation, especially one requiring dedication. Sometimes the word is used to distinguish one's main occupation from one's hobby (avocation), and the word is used to suggest a calling: "By inclination and circumstance, she found that the ministry was the *vocation* for her."

CARPET/RUG (N.)

Both terms designate fabric covering for floors, but in careful usage *carpet* is the term for what completely covers a floor and *rug* is the term for what covers only part of a floor: "I prefer wall-to-wall *carpets* to throw *rugs*."

CART/WAGON (N.)

A *cart* usually designates any two-wheeled vehicle drawn by a horse, mule, ox, or dog. A *cart* can be heavy or light and is usually uncovered: "The horse drew the *cart* filled with farming supplies."

A *wagon*, when distinguished from a *cart*, has four wheels, is usually open (except when it is a covered *wagon*), and is usually pulled by horses. The word can also refer to a low four-wheeled vehicle made as a toy for children: "The *wagon* with the bulk commodities was drawn by a horse."

CASTIGATE/CHASTEN/CHASTISE (V.)

To *castigate* is to reprimand (often publicly) by tongue or pen: "The minister *castigated* his parishioner for adultery."

To *chasten* people usually implies subjecting them to affliction not so much to punish them as to test, humble, and purify them: "The painful consequences of her act *chastened* her."

To *chastise* people can involve corporal punishment, sometimes inflicted in anger though often inflicted to reform: "Sarah *chastises* her children by spanking them."

Chastise can, however, also be used to mean "censure severely in an attempt to correct," in which usage its meaning is close to that of *castigate*.

CASUALTY/FATALITY (N.)

When *casualty* refers to a person, it describes someone who has been seriously injured or killed, as by an act of violence or act of nature: "A *casualty* of war is an injured or dead member of the armed forces."

A *fatality*, when the word refers to the condition of a

person, describes a death, regardless of its cause: "The automobile accident resulted in two *fatalities*."

CATEGORIAL/CATEGORICAL (ADJ.)

Categorial means "pertaining to categories": "The Dewey Decimal System draws *categorial* distinctions between fiction and nonfiction library books."

Categorical means "unconditional" or "unqualified": "When we asked the man to donate five dollars to our cause, he gave us a *categorical* no."

CELEBRATION/JAMBOREE/PARTY (N.)

A *celebration* commemorates a special day or event, typically longer and larger than a party and often including scheduled events or ceremonies: "We enjoyed the toasts during the couple's anniversary *celebration*."

A *jamboree* is a large-scale planned celebration consisting of various events and entertainments, especially of the Boy Scouts or Girl Scouts: "A *jamboree* is normally a noisy, festive celebration."

A *party* is an occasion on which people assemble for social interaction, entertainment, and often refreshments: "We needed to rush if we were to arrive on time for the dinner *party*."

CEMENT/CONCRETE (N.)

Cement is an adhesive of clay and rock materials forming a paste when it is mixed with water. *Concrete* is a construction material containing such ingredients as gravel, slag, and pebbles held together by *cement*: "The workers were careful to put enough *cement* into the *concrete* mixture."

CENSOR/CENSURE/EXPURGATE (V.)

To *censor* is to examine such things as documents, movies, music, and TV programs to suppress, alter, or remove anything considered obscene, offensive, libelous, or dangerous: "Television executives decided to *censor* remarks some comedians made about the Vietnam conflict."

To *censure* is to find fault with and to criticize as blameworthy or to express public and official disapproval of: "A group of parents *censured* the record company for allowing the obscene lyrics."

To *expurgate* involves allowing something to be published or displayed but only after it has been purged of what is considered offensive, harmful, or erroneous: "The book was *expurgated* to make it appropriate for children."

CEREMONIAL/CEREMONIOUS (ADJ.)

Ceremonial refers to things associated with ceremonies: "The awards were given during a *ceremonial* dinner."

Ceremonious refers to people and things associated with ceremonies, especially when connected with pomp and formality (including excessive formality): "The speaker's *ceremonious* diction and pronunciation were so affected as to be pompous."

CHAFE/CHAFF (V.)

Chafe means "to rub so as to wear away; to irritate, annoy, or vex": "The rough speech of the children *chafed* their teacher."

Chaff is a verb meaning "to make fun of or joke about someone or something; to jest or banter": "They *chaffed* me for wearing a pink tie."

CHARY/WARY (ADJ.)

A *chary* person is discreetly cautious, either somewhat hesitant and vigilant about risks and dangers, or shy or reserved (as when accepting compliments or speaking openly): "Sam was a *chary* investor."

A *wary* person is suspiciously alert to danger, difficulty, or possible loss, and cunning in escaping or evading it: "The *wary* soldier had a remarkable ability to detect and avoid danger."

CHEST/DRESSER (N.)

A *chest* (or *chest* of drawers) is a piece of storage furniture with drawers, typically used for clothing: "The *chest* contained many of my clothes."

A *dresser* is a *chest* with a mirror attached to it: "I liked to put on my necktie in front of the *dresser*."

CHILDISH/CHILDLIKE (ADJ.)

Childish behavior is marked by immaturity or simplemindedness: "I have little patience for *childish* temper tantrums."

Childlike behavior is marked by innocence, trust, and frankness: "My sister takes a *childlike* pleasure in opening birthday gifts."

In short, the word *childish* is a term of reproach, whereas the word *childlike* refers to what are normally considered the endearing characteristics of children.

CITE/QUOTE (V.)

To *cite* is to mention or name an example, proof, precedent, or source: "I can *cite* the precedent for the case."

To *quote* some source is to speak or write the source's

words verbatim: "My footnotes *cited* several references, but I *quoted* only a few of them."

CLAIRVOYANCE/ESP/PRECOGNITION/ TELEPATHY (N.)

Clairvoyance applies to the act or power professed by certain persons of discerning objects hidden from sight or far away: "Remote viewing, if it exists, involves *clairvoyance*."

ESP, or extrasensory perception, is any communication with or awareness of phenomena beyond the reach of the five senses: "The scientist believes that there is no convincing evidence that *ESP* can reliably yield knowledge in the way that sensory experience can."

Precognition refers to knowledge of future events: "Some people believe that dreams can be instruments of *precognition*."

Telepathy is communication between minds without the channels of senses: "The psychic claimed that through *telepathy*, she could know what people were thinking."

CLAW/TALON (N.)

A *claw* is a sharp toenail on the foot of an animal or the pincers of lobsters or crabs: "The cat's right front *claw* scratched me."

A *talon* is the *claw* of a bird of prey: "A hawk will seize its prey in its *talons*."

CLENCH/CLINCH (V.)

To *clench* is to hold, grip, or shut tightly: "Michelle's nervousness caused her to *clench* the arms of the chair."

To *clinch* is to settle or make final, definite, or beyond dispute, as when one *clinches* an argument or a sale: "His citing the *Oxford English Dictionary clinched* the verbal dispute."

Note that *clinch* can also mean "to grasp and struggle at close quarters (as in wrestling)" or "to hold an opponent at close quarters by the arms or around the waist (as in boxing)."

CLIENT/CUSTOMER (N.)

A *client* is a person who engages the professional advice or services of another, whereas a *customer* is a patron of a merchant or shopkeeper. "A lawyer has *clients*, and a person who eats at MacDonald's is a *customer*."

Some people regard the distinction as somewhat arbitrary and snobbish, because a woman who pays one hundred dollars to have her hair done is probably called a *client*, whereas a man who pays fifteen dollars for a haircut is a *customer*.

CLIMACTIC/CLIMATIC (ADJ.)

Climactic means "having to do with a climax": "The criminal was caught during the *climactic* movie scene."

Climatic means "having to do with climate": "The *climatic* change from Louisiana to Arizona was beneficial for my grandmother, who had difficulty breathing in extreme humidity."

CLUB SODA/SELTZER/TONIC WATER (N.)

Club soda (or soda water) is a flavorless soft drink consisting of plain water into which carbon dioxide has been dissolved. Although *club soda* can simply be carbonated water, it may contain (and in the United Kingdom normally does contain) sodium bicarbonate (baking soda): "The mixed drink called for *club soda*."

Seltzer (or *seltzer* water) is a flavorless effervescent beverage named after Niederselters, a German town where the waters occur naturally. The term can describe naturally fizzy mineral water or water infused with carbon dioxide: "In the mid-1800s, flavors were added to *seltzer*, a process that led to soft drinks."

Tonic water is a sweetened beverage in which carbonated water has been flavored with quinine, a bark extract: "Although *tonic water* has become a popular mixer for gin or vodka, it was invented by the British in India as a pleasant way of taking a daily dose of quinine to prevent malaria."

COHERENT/COHESIVE (ADJ.)

What is *coherent* is logically consistent or something whose parts constitute a harmonious whole: "His story was plausible and entirely *coherent*."

Something that is *cohesive* sticks or works together: "A good glue, like a good sports team, should be *cohesive*."

COLLAGE/MONTAGE (N.)

A *collage* is an artistic composition of various materials (such as paper, cloth, or wood) not usually associated with one another glued on a surface: "Because artistic *collages* contain diverse elements, the word *collage* can describe a hodgepodge."

A *montage*, when it's distinguishable from a *collage*,

is a photographic or cinematographic work in which similar elements from various sources are juxtaposed, superimposed, or otherwise combined: "*Montages* will contain different items, such as different photographs or pictures, organized in such a way as to suggest common themes."

COLOGNE/EAU DE TOILETTE/PERFUME (N.)

Cologne, or originally and more properly *eau de Cologne* (French for "water of Cologne"), is a toiletry and type of light perfume that originated in Cologne, Germany, and is nowadays a generic term defining scented formulations by a typical concentration of 2 to 5 percent essential oils: "Napoleon loved *cologne* and popularized it in France, supposedly using about eight quarts a month."

Eau de toilette is stronger than *cologne* but weaker than *perfume* and often has 4 to 10 percent of essential oils (aromatic essence), though it can sometimes have higher concentrations: "Designed to be splashed over the body in the morning to awaken and refresh, *eau de toilette* is the scent best suited for everyday use."

Perfume has the highest concentration of essential oils, often 25 percent, though possibly 30 or even 40 percent. It has the least amount of alcohol and is the purest and most expensive of all scents: "She dabbed on her *perfume*, which would last for six hours."

COMET/METEOR/METEORITE/
METEOROID (N.)

Comets revolve around the Sun; are made up of ice, frozen gases (especially carbon dioxide and methane), and rock; and don't crash into the Earth: "Halley's *Comet*, visible from Earth every seventy-five to seventy-six years, is probably the most famous *comet*."

Meteors are solid chunks of rock and metal, producing light from friction as they enter the Earth's atmosphere. When they are outside the Earth's atmosphere, they are called *meteoroids*. A *meteoroid* that enters our atmosphere and strikes our planet is called a *meteorite*: "Many *meteors* don't become *meteoroids*, and many *meteoroids* burn up before hitting the Earth and therefore never become *meteorites*."

COMMON/MUTUAL (ADJ.)

To the extent that the two terms have distinct meanings, *common* relates to what two or more persons do together or share alike: "My friend and I have *common* interests."

Mutual includes the idea of reciprocity, describing something done or felt, for example, by each of two persons toward the other: "My friend and I have *mutual* respect—in other words, my friend and I respect each other."

COMMUNIQUÉ/EPISTLE/MEMORANDUM/ MISSIVE (N.)

A *communiqué* can often apply to a brief news item intended for immediate publication or broadcast: "The dictator would rarely speak in public but would have subordinates issue *communiqués*."

An *epistle* is a formal or elegant letter: "The note was too brief and poorly written to qualify as an *epistle*."

A *memorandum* is a presentation of data used chiefly

in business or bureaucracies for an informal communication: "The executive sent a *memorandum* to all the employees explaining the new safety rules."

A *missive* often refers to a formal or an official letter. Originally, a letter *missive* was a letter from a superior authority addressed to a particular person or group and conveying a command, recommendation, permission, or invitation: "*Missives* are often formal, official letters; thus, calling brief, personal, and poorly written letters *missives* may suggest irony or condescension."

COMPEL/IMPEL (V.)

Both words mean "to force into action," but *compel* suggests the application of external force over which one has no control. "When someone is threatened with a gun, she may be *compelled* to hand over her money."

Impel, in contrast, implies that the force comes from within oneself: "Her conscience *impelled* her to oppose the laws enforcing racial segregation."

COMPLACENT/COMPLAISANT/ COMPLIANT (ADJ.)

If you're *complacent*, you're smug or self-satisfied: "The people were *complacent* when they should have been self-critical."

If you're *complaisant*, you're eager to please: "The political candidate was cooperative because he was *complaisant*."

If you're *compliant*, you're submissive or obedient: "It is wise to be *compliant* when receiving directives from police officers."

COMPLEMENT/COMPLIMENT (V.)

Although *complement* and *compliment* can be used as nouns or verbs, one can understand their use as nouns by understanding their use as verbs.

The verb *complement* means "to complete": "The dessert *complemented* the meal."

The verb *compliment* means "to praise": "I want to *compliment* you for creating the delicious dessert."

COMPLEMENT/SUPPLEMENT (N.)

A *complement* is what makes something complete: "The necktie is the perfect *complement* to your suit."

A *supplement* is what is added, as something extra, to something already complete: "The wages from my part-time job are a *supplement* to my usual income."

COMPOST/MULCH (N.)

Compost is a mixture consisting of decayed organic matter (such as leaves and manure) used as fertilizer: "We knew that the *compost* was needed as a fertilizer, but we didn't like its smell."

Mulch is a protective covering (such as sawdust, leaves, straw, manure, or a combination thereof) spread on the ground before rotting to hold moisture, maintain even soil temperatures, control weeds, provide a decorative appearance, or sometimes to prevent erosion or enrich the soil: "The most popular *mulch* nowadays includes hardwood, cypress, pine bark, pine needles, and cedar."

COMPULSION/OBSESSION (N.)

Compulsion refers to behavior that drives people to act against their wishes or better judgment. One has *compulsions* to do things: "Despite knowing that he was overweight, Bobby had a *compulsion* to eat the ice cream."

Obsession refers to ideas or beliefs dominating or haunting people's consciousness; an inescapable preoccupation with ideas or feelings (especially when they are known to be unreasonable): "The man's sense of being unworthy in the sight of God became an *obsession*."

CONCERT/RECITAL (N.)

A *concert* is a musical performance by a group, whereas a *recital* is a musical performance by a soloist or two performers, the soloist and an accompanist: "On Monday, we enjoyed the rock *concert*, and on Tuesday, we enjoyed Yo Yo Ma's cello *recital*."

Note that sometimes the word *recital* refers to an exhibition *concert* given by dance students.

CONCLAVE/MEETING (N.)

A *conclave* is a private or secret gathering; a *meeting* is an arranged gathering: "A group of Roman Catholic cardinals convened a *conclave* to select the next pope, which made for an unusual *meeting*."

CONDEMN/CONTEMN (V.)

To *condemn* is to pronounce as ill advised, evil, reprehensible, or wrong, typically after a final or definitive judgment: "We have no choice but to *condemn* genocide."

To *contemn* is to view or treat with contempt; to reject with disdain: "The radio talk show host *contemned* political leftists, regarding them as undermining civilization."

CONDITION/PRECONDITION (N.)

A *condition* is a requirement for something: "It is a *condition* of some academic courses that students attend a minimum number of classes."

A *precondition* is something that must exist before something else can occur; a condition needed in advance: "It is a *precondition* that students taking four-hundred-level philosophy courses should have already taken lower-level philosophy courses."

CONDOLE/CONSOLE (V.)

To *condole*, which is always followed by *with*, is to express sympathy: "We *condoled* with the widow."

To *console* is to comfort—that is, to offer solace or consolation: "Her grief was difficult to *console*."

CONFOUND/CONFUSE (V.)

Normally, the word *confound* implies a temporary mental paralysis produced by astonishment or amazement: "The soldiers *confounded* their enemies by rapid and unpredictable maneuvers."

Someone *confused* is perplexed, bewildered, or unclear in mind: "We were *confused* by the man's vague and ambiguous directions."

CONNOTATION/DENOTATION (N.)

Connotation refers to meaning that is influenced by personal experience, cultural associations, or both, which tend to color the sense of the word by how people feel about it: "The expression 'apple pie,' for many people, carries a *connotation* of America, including what many people view as American wholesomeness."

Denotation designates the generally accepted meaning of a word, apart from any emotional associations: "The expression 'Bible-believing Christian' has a fairly specific descriptive meaning, or *denotation*."

CONSTRAIN/RESTRAIN (V.)

Constrain means "to compel by physical, moral, or circumstantial force": "She was *constrained* to agree with the demonstrable truth."

To *restrain* is to hold back or keep in check: "He found it difficult to *restrain* his curiosity."

CONTAGIOUS/INFECTIOUS (ADJ.)

A *contagious* disease is spread from person to person by direct or indirect contact or spread from one species to another: "The sexually transmitted disease gonorrhea is an example of a *contagious* disease."

Infectious diseases result from the presence of pathogenic microbes, such as viruses, bacteria, fungi, protozoa, and parasites. *Infectious* diseases may involve but don't require human contact: "His diarrhea was due to an *infectious* disease."

CONTEMPORARY/MODERN (ADJ.)

Something *contemporary* is of the same period: "The author and scientist Francis Bacon was *contemporary* with Shakespeare."

Something *modern* is of the present time or of what has existed or occurred from some point in the past to the present: "*Modern* Greek has existed since roughly the sixteenth century."

CONTEMPT/DISDAIN (V.)

An attitude of *contempt* is one of despising or holding in disrespect: "We have nothing but *contempt* for racism."

An attitude of *disdain* is one of haughty disrespect, in which one looks down on the object of *disdain* with aloof superiority: "The prophet had *disdain* for hypocritical priests."

CONTEMPTIBLE/CONTEMPTUOUS (ADJ.)

What is *contemptible* deserves contempt: "Anyone who is cruel to a pet is *contemptible*."

What is *contemptuous* feels or expresses contempt: "The worker's *contemptuous* attitude toward authority alienated his supervisor."

CONTINUAL/CONTINUOUS (ADJ.)

A *continual* event recurs at intervals, often with brief but regular intermissions in time: "Between the morning and the evening, I received *continual* phone calls."

A *continuous* event occurs without interruption: "A clock's ticking is *continuous*."

CONTRADICTORY/CONTRARY (ADJ.)

Contradictory implies the denial of some term, proposition, or principle. When proposition A is logically *contradictory* to proposition B, the truth of one implies the falsity of the other: "In logic, a set of two propositions that are *contradictory* will contain exactly one true proposition and exactly one false proposition: (1) 'All human beings are mammals.' (2) 'Some human beings are not mammals.'"

Contrary intentions, motives, and opinions normally have no common ground and are diametrically opposed: "In logic, *contraries* are poles apart; if proposition A is *contrary* to proposition B, they cannot both be true, but they can both be false: (1) 'All Americans are wealthy.' (2) 'All Americans are poor.'"

CONVINCE/PERSUADE (ADJ.)

Convince means "to bring or cause to have belief, acceptance, or conviction": "I *convinced* my friend that parts of Virginia are west of West Virginia."

Persuade can mean "to bring to belief," but it can also mean and often does mean "to win over to a course of action." Accordingly, *persuade* is often followed by the infinitive, whereas *convince* should never be followed by an infinitive: "I *persuaded* [not *convinced*] her to go with me."

COPIOUS/FULSOME (ADJ.)

Anything *copious* is plentiful: "The learned book contained *copious* footnotes."

Something *fulsome* is disgustingly excessive or overdone: "The politician's *fulsome* praise turned off many listeners."

COPY/REPLICA (N.)

A *copy* is an imitation, transcript, or reproduction of an original work (as of an article, a letter, or a painting): "I made a *copy* of your notes."

Although a *replica* can be a facsimile of an original work (including a work of art), it often describes a reproduction or facsimile made by the maker of the original or under the maker's direction: "The sculptor produced a *replica* of his statue."

CORONET/CROWN/DIADEM/TIARA (N.)

A *coronet* is a small crown, without jewels, worn by princes, nobles, or peers: "The *coronet* the prince wore was less ornate than the king's *crown*."

A *crown* is headgear symbolizing political sovereignty, entirely circling the head, normally bejeweled, and with a top, often of velvet: "The king wore an ornate *crown*."

A *diadem* resembles a *crown* but has no top, making it a royal headband: "Anglo-Saxon kings wore *diadems*."

A *tiara* is a bejeweled or flowered headband or semicircle for formal wear worn by women or the three-tiered headgear formerly worn by the pope: "Grace Kelly looked stunning with or without her *tiara*." "In the Roman Catholic Church, the papal *tiara* was a high cap surrounded by three *crowns* and bearing a globe surmounted by a cross."

CORRESPONDINGLY/SIMILARLY (ADV.)

Two things *correspondingly* related are connected in a matching way: "If people's incomes are increased, their expenses often *correspondingly* increase."

Two things *similarly* related are comparably connected: "Both of us were *similarly* disappointed."

CORROBORATE/VERIFY (V.)

To *corroborate* a belief is to provide evidence for the truth of it. To *verify* a belief is to prove it to be true: "Since one witness's statement can *corroborate* another witness's statement and still be false because the corroborating witness is lying or mistaken, one can *verify* only what is true."

CORRODE/ERODE (V.)

To *corrode* is to eat away by degrees, as if by gnawing, or to eat away or diminish by acid or alkali reaction or chemical alteration: "The acid will *corrode* the material."

To *erode* is to wear away gradually, especially (but not only) by rubbing or the movement of water: "The river *eroded* the shore."

Note that your confidence in someone may *erode* but not *corrode*.

COUNCIL/COUNSEL (N.)

A *council* is a group of people who meet to make decisions in matters of government, religion, or athletics: "The city *council* met to discuss congestion pricing."

Counsel is advice (or instruction) or one providing advice (as a lawyer, who provides legal *counsel*): "Bob's wife gave him wise *counsel* about asking for a raise."

COVER-UP/WHITEWASH (N.)

A *cover-up* tries to prevent an investigation or exposure of some action: "A *cover-up* can become more serious legally and politically than the action covered up."

A *whitewash* is an attempt to absolve someone from blame by specious or deceptive means, especially lying. The term comes from a mixture of lime and water once used for whitening walls and woodwork: "No *whitewash* of President Nixon's Watergate scandal would have been successful."

CRANIUM/SKULL (N.)

The *cranium* is the part of the *skull* enclosing the brain, consisting of all the bones of the *skull* except one—the inferior maxillary, or mandible (the lower jaw): "His *cranium* wasn't strong enough to prevent the concussion."

The *skull* is the bony framework of the head, thirteen bones enclosing the brain and supporting the flesh, scalp, and elements of the face: "One of the main functions of the *skull* is to protect the brain."

CREVASSE/CREVICE (N.)

A *crevasse* is a deep cleft in a glacier: "We advise against skiing near a *crevasse*."

A *crevice* is a narrow crack or small fissure in rock, wall, ice, and so on: "We were unhappy to see some roaches crawl out of a *crevice* in the wall."

CRISIS/EMERGENCY (N.)

A *crisis* is a turning point for better or worse, a decisive moment, or an unsettled time or state of affairs: "The sudden change in the patient's breathing and heart constituted a *crisis*."

An *emergency* is an unforeseen circumstance calling for immediate action: "The power outages and damage to the local hospital created *emergencies*."

CRITIQUE/REVIEW (N.)

A *critique*, written or spoken, evaluates a work, especially one literary or scholarly. It is supposed to be reasonably objective and can contain suggestions for improvement, often proposed by friends or colleagues. A *critique* can be of a work in progress and be designed to refine it for publication, or it can be an oral or written evaluation of a scholarly paper delivered to a scholarly society or association: "The graduate student presented a *critique* of another student's paper."

A *review*, as of a book or movie, is normally an evaluation of a finished product—something already produced, performed, or published. It is often generally favorable or unfavorable, often doesn't even pretend to be unbiased, and can even display hostility: "The *review* by the movie critic was entertaining but caustic."

CROTCH/GROIN/LOINS (N.)

The *crotch* is the area formed by the joint of two legs or limbs, as on the human body, a pair of pants, or a tree: "The pants had a tear in the *crotch*."

The *groin* is the hollow of the body where the abdomen meets the hip: "He suffered a *groin* injury."

The *loins* are between the lowest ribs and the hip bone, both front and back: "The *loins*, unlike the *crotch* or *groin*, include the reproductive organs."

CRYPT/MAUSOLEUM/SEPULCHER/VAULT (N.)

A *crypt* is a chamber wholly or partly underground, but when it contains a *vault* (a chamber housing a coffin), a *crypt* is found under the main floor of a church: "The man's great-grandfather was buried in a *crypt* in an old church."

A *mausoleum* is usually a stone building with places for entombing the dead above ground: "Grant's Tomb is a *mausoleum* in New York City, containing the bodies of Ulysses S. Grant and his wife, Julia Dent Grant."

A *sepulcher* can describe any chamber used as a grave,

though it can also designate a structure or a recess in some old churches in which the Eucharist was deposited during ceremonies on Good Friday and taken out at Easter: "We discovered that the body was buried in a *sepulcher* on holy ground."

A *vault* can be a place underground for keeping the dead, a part of a cellar devoted to a special purpose (such as storing wine), or a place above or below ground where money and other valuables are stored: "The thieves removed the jewelry from the *vault*."

CUCKOLD/WITTOL (N.)

A *cuckold* is a man whose wife has been unfaithful to him: "Some *cuckolds* know about their wives' infidelity, but others don't."

A *wittol* is someone who knows that his wife is being unfaithful and acquiesces in the infidelity—that is, a *wittol* is a tame *cuckold*: "The *wittol* tolerated his wife's infidelity because he liked her money more than he disliked her infidelity."

CULTIVATED/CULTURED (ADJ.)

In *cultivated* usage, *cultivated* modifies minds, tastes, speech, or behavior, and *cultured* modifies persons and pearls: "A person may have a *cultivated* mind in the sense of being highly trained and developed without necessarily being a *cultured* person in the sense of having refined tastes."

CYNIC/PESSIMIST/SKEPTIC (N.)

A *cynic* tends to believe that people are motivated wholly by self-interest and expects the worst of them:

"A *cynic* usually believes that behind socially acceptable explanations lie socially unacceptable motives."

A *pessimist* doesn't just distrust human nature but is inclined to have a negative opinion of everything, believing that reality is ultimately evil, or as evil as it can conceivably be: "The *pessimist* didn't want to try to win a million dollars because he felt sure that his problems would simply be magnified."

A *skeptic* is a person who is inclined to question what others rarely, if ever, question. People can be skeptical about religion, ESP, or even the possibility of any knowledge: "The religious *skeptics* insisted on evidence alone rather than faith for finding truth."

D

DAPPLED/PIEBALD/SKEWBALD (ADJ.)

Dappled, *piebald*, and *skewbald* are usually applied to animals, especially horses.

Dappled means "spotted" or, more specifically, "marked with small spots, patches, or dots contrasting in color or shade with the background": "The *dappled* horse was white with brown patches."

Piebald can describe something with two different colors but applies especially to animals that are spotted or blotched with black and white: "The *piebald* horse had more white than black."

Skewbald animals have spots or patches of white on a nonblack coat: "Because the horse's spots were white on a brown coat, the horse was *skewbald*."

DARK AGES/MIDDLE AGES (N.)

The expression *Dark Ages* is an old term for the historical period from about the year 400 CE to about the year 1000 CE: "The creators of the expression *Dark Ages* considered that period unenlightened."

The *Middle Ages* extend from the fifth to the fifteenth centuries: "The *Middle Ages* received the name because the period so described was thought to fall between ancient and modern times."

DAZED/DAZZLED (V.)

A *dazed* person has been stunned, stupefied, or bewildered, as by a literal blow to the head or by bad news: "She was *dazed* by the death of her mother."

A *dazzled* person has been overpowered or blinded by strong light or by a brilliant display of skill: "The pianist *dazzled* us with his performance."

DEBAR/DISBAR (V.)

To *debar* is to exclude: "She was *debarred* from the contest because she worked for the sponsor."

To *disbar* is to expel a lawyer from practice: "The lawyer was *disbarred* because of his felony conviction."

DECEITFUL/DECEPTIVE (ADJ.)

Deceitful is stronger than *deceptive* and implies intentional dishonesty: "The *deceitful* boy had concocted the story to avoid going to school."

Deceptive describes whatever has the power to mislead, though it can describe what tends to deceive: "The ice on the lake was *deceptive* because it seemed sturdier than it was."

DECIDED/DECISIVE (ADJ.)

What is *decided* is unmistakable: "She has a *decided* Bostonian accent."

What is *decisive* is conclusive or deciding: "Her lead in the first five races proved *decisive* in the sailing regatta."

DECIDUOUS/EVERGREEN (ADJ.)

What is *deciduous* falls off or is shed at the end of the growing period, as leaves, fruit, or teeth: "The *deciduous* trees lost their leaves for part of the year."

An *evergreen* plant has leaves all year round: "Most species of conifers (such as white pine, red cedar, and blue spruce) are *evergreen* plants."

DECRY/DESCRY (V.)

To *decry* is to criticize somebody or something strongly and publicly: "The senator *decried* corporate fraud."

To *descry* is to catch sight of (especially something difficult to discern): "The sailor had excellent vision and was able to *descry* the lighthouse from a great distance."

DEDUCTIVE REASONING/INDUCTIVE REASONING (N.)

Deductive reasoning is the kind of reasoning in which the conclusion is presented as necessitated or logically implied by previously known or given data (the premises). In a valid deductive argument, to assert the premises while denying the conclusion would be self-contradictory: "Geometry typifies *deductive reasoning.*"

Inductive reasoning is the kind of reasoning in which the conclusion is presented as probably true, given the truth of the premises. Inductive arguments come in varying strengths, depending on how strongly the premises support the probable truth of the conclusion: "Weather prediction relies heavily on *inductive reasoning.*"

DEFECTIVE/DEFICIENT (ADJ.)

What is *defective* has a defect or fault: "The car tire was *defective* when I bought it."

What is *deficient* lacks something it should have: "Her diet was *deficient* in green vegetables."

DEFINITE/DEFINITIVE (ADJ.)

What is *definite* is clear, unambiguous, precisely defined: "We need a *definite* deadline to achieve the goal."

What is *definitive* is conclusive or authoritative: "We agreed that we'd treat whatever *Webster's Third New International Dictionary* says about the word's origin as *definitive*."

DEJECTED/DEPRESSED (ADJ.)

Dejected applies to feelings, frustration, or discouragement that may be brief and occasioned by some event: "His *dejected* look disappeared as soon as he found that he was going on the trip."

Depressed often applies to a lingering sadness, moodiness, or brooding, as distinguished from a brief negative mood in response to some event: "The *depressed* woman was used to being sad."

DELAY/POSTPONE (V.)

To *delay* is to lay something aside, to impede, or to put something off: "The man decided to *delay* his trip until it would be more convenient."

To *postpone* is to put something off with the intention of taking it up again at a definite future time: "The game was *postponed* until next Saturday."

DELIBERATE/INTENTIONAL (ADJ.)

A *deliberate* act is thoroughly and carefully thought through: "Your decision must not be hasty but *deliberate*."

An *intentional* act is something one does on purpose or by design: "The act was no accident but *intentional*."

DELIMIT/LIMIT (V.)

To *delimit* is to mark off boundaries, or to separate by fixing dividing lines: "The law *delimits* police powers."

To *limit* is to restrict or contain: "Please *limit* your questions to budgetary matters."

DELUGE/FLOOD (N.)

A *deluge* is an overflowing of land by water, especially from continuous rain or a burst dam: "The continuous rain produced a *deluge* in parts of downtown Norfolk, Virginia."

A *flood* implies the flowing of water, often in abundance, over land not usually submerged, as by a swollen stream or river or a burst water main: "The rising rivers produced *floods* in low-lying areas."

DELUSION/ILLUSION (N.)

A *delusion* is a false belief, especially one held because of self-deception, and sometimes held despite indisputable contrary evidence: "He has *delusions* of grandeur."

An *illusion* can describe anything that deceives or misleads people, including a false belief, a misleading sensory image, or an unreal image: "The magician was adept at creating optical and other *illusions*."

DENIGRATE/DISPARAGE (V.)

Denigrate literally means "to blacken" and describes defaming people's characters or reputation: "His reputation was seriously damaged when his enemy *denigrated* it."

Disparage means "to speak slightingly of" or "to run down," minimizing or devaluing someone's character or achievements, especially indirectly, as through insinuation, invidious comparisons, or faint praise: "When people *disparage* others' accomplishments, they suggest that those accomplishments are less valuable than many think."

DEPARTMENT/DIVISION (N.)

A *department* is a distinct branch or section of a government, business, university, and so on. A *department* is more or less autonomous and is more nearly independent than a *division*: "A shoe *department* of a department store has little to do with the automotive *department*."

A *division* is a small part of a whole whose parts are closely interrelated: "The *division* was closely regulated by its parent company and dependent on it for advertising, direction, distribution, and so on."

DEPOSITORY/REPOSITORY (N.)

A *depository* is a storehouse where something valuable is deposited: "The *depository* contained much furniture and some valuable jewelry."

A *repository* can designate a storehouse, though usually one smaller than that designated by *depository*. More often, however, a *repository* is a person or thing storing something nonphysical, such as secrets, information, knowledge, or wisdom: "A dictionary is a *repository* of knowledge."

DEPRECATE/DEPRECIATE (V.)

To *deprecate* is to express disapproval: "The woman decided to *deprecate* her son's decision to live with his fiancée."

To *depreciate* is to belittle or reduce in value: "His mother *depreciated* his decision to spend his money on a new car, whose value would soon *depreciate*."

When people talk of "self-*deprecating* humor," they mean "self-*depreciating* humor," in which people belittle themselves.

DERISIVE/DERISORY (ADJ.)

Derisive means "showing contempt," "expressing derision," "mocking," or "jeering": "The *derisive* tone of the boy's answer displayed contempt for his teacher."

Derisory, like *derisive*, means "expressing contempt," but often means "laughable" or "laughably small": "The salary for adjunct college professors is so low as to be *derisory*."

DESPAIRING/DESPONDENT (ADJ.)

Anyone *despairing* feels completely hopeless: "Sadly, many unpopular high school students graduate while *despairing* of their future."

Anyone *despondent* is low in spirits but not necessarily devoid of hope: "The student became *despondent* when he was rejected by his first college choice."

DESPISE/HATE (V.)

To *despise* is to look down on with scorn, contempt, or extreme dislike: "The industrious man *despised* lazy people."

To *hate* is to dislike intensely but needn't imply "looking down on": "A man may *hate* another man for running away with his wife without *despising* him."

DIAGNOSIS/PROGNOSIS (N.)

A *diagnosis* says what's wrong with you. "The doctor's *diagnosis* was based on evaluating symptoms, laboratory tests, and x-rays."

A *prognosis* predicts how things will turn out: "Because the tumor was benign, the *prognosis* was favorable."

DINNER/SUPPER (N.)

Dinner describes the main meal of the day, which in rural areas was traditionally served at midday to supply energy to farm workers. Many people who eat their main meal at midday and eat a lighter meal shortly before bedtime will sometimes call the lighter meal *supper*: "Strictly speaking, Americans who have their main meal at night are eating *dinner*, not *supper*."

DISBELIEVER/UNBELIEVER (N.)

Both terms designate those without religious belief, though *disbeliever* carries a stronger sense of positive rejection of religion, and *unbeliever* carries a sense of neutral abstention from religion: "The militant atheist was a vocal *disbeliever*, who saw agnostics as *unbelievers* lacking the courage necessary for positive disbelief."

DISCOMFITURE/DISCOMFORT (N.)

Discomfiture is a state of being frustrated, foiled, or confused: "The coach's *discomfiture* came from several consecutive losses."

Discomfort is a lack of comfort, or mental or physical distress: "Her *discomfort* was due to her not knowing what to expect at the job interview."

DISCOVER/INVENT (V.)

To *discover* is to find something: "We *discovered* a new restaurant."

To *invent* is to devise or create something: "Benjamin Franklin *invented* bifocals."

DISCREET/DISCRETE (ADJ.)

To be *discreet* is to show prudence and wise self-restraint in speech or behavior: "We advised our friend to be *discreet* when disagreeing with his supervisor."

To be *discrete* is to be separate and distinct: "Her two objections to the proposal are quite different and need to be kept *discrete*."

DISCREPANCY/DISPARITY (N.)

A *discrepancy* is a disagreement or inconsistency: "There were *discrepancies* between the two eyewitness accounts."

A *disparity* is a difference in degree, as in rank, grade, age, or condition: "The *disparity* between the richest people and the poorest people is large."

DISEASE/ILLNESS (N.)

Disease in its usual and broadest use implies an impairment of the normal state of a living body, as defined by objective criteria determined by physicians: "The person's heart definitely showed signs of *disease*."

Illness can be a synonym of *disease*, but it also has a more subjective use, based on how a person feels: "Although she didn't have a *disease*, she called her unpleasant feeling an *illness*."

DISINTERESTED/UNINTERESTED (ADJ.)

A *disinterested* person is free from bias: "A judge is supposed to be *disinterested*."

An *uninterested* person lacks concern and is indifferent, without mental or emotional engagement: "She was *uninterested* in returning to school."

DISPEL/DISPERSE/DISSIPATE (V.)

To *dispel* is to drive away, as if by swatting: "We can *dispel* that false notion by advancing solid advice that disproves it."

To *disperse* usually implies widely spreading something completely broken up: "The police decided to *disperse* the crowd."

The word *dissipate* stresses the idea of completely disintegrating or dissolving some mass or whole: "We feared that he would *dissipate* his inheritance and have nothing for retirement."

DISSATISFIED/UNSATISFIED (ADJ.)

If you're *dissatisfied*, you are displeased or disappointed. If you are *unsatisfied*, you lack complete fulfillment: "If a meal leaves you *dissatisfied*, you positively disliked it; if it left you *unsatisfied*, you wanted more of it."

DISSENSION/DISSENT/DISSIDENCE (N.)

Dissension is likely to emphasize disharmony and noisy antipathy between groups, creating hostile factions: "The *dissension* among the three groups led to shouting."

Dissent suggests a difference of opinion, as between a member of a group and the majority: "The justice's opinion constituted *dissent* from the majority opinion."

Dissidence suggests strong disagreement with established government or other general opinion: "Stalin ruthlessly suppressed any *dissidence*."

DISSIMULATE/SIMULATE (V.)

To *dissimulate* is to conceal or hide under a false appearance: "He couldn't *dissimulate* his true motives."

To *simulate* is to pretend: "The girl decided to *simulate* being ill to get out of going to school."

DISSIPATED/DISSOLUTE (ADJ.)

A *dissipated* person has lost self-control in pursuit of pleasure and consequently suffers in health: "The late hours and constant drinking caught up with the *dissipated* man."

A *dissolute* person is unrestrained or lawless in conduct, especially in sexual conduct: "The minister told us that a politician's *dissolute* lifestyle can adversely influence his official duties."

DISTRUST/MISTRUST (V.)

Distrust normally implies a stronger belief that something is wrong than *mistrust*. Often *distrust* suggests a belief in another's guilt, treachery, or weakness:

"Because the members of the jury trusted the witnesses for the prosecution but *distrusted* those for the defense, they decided to convict the defendant."

To *mistrust* is to regard with suspicion or to lack confidence in: "His parents *mistrusted* his ability to make sound decisions."

Note that *mistrust* is normally preferred in describing self-doubt: "I *mistrust* myself" is more idiomatic than "I *distrust* myself."

DISTURB/PERTURB (V.)

To *disturb* people is to interfere with or break up their tranquillity: "When I'm relaxing, I don't want to be *disturbed.*"

To *perturb* is to make uneasy or to cause to be upset, worried, or alarmed: "A good-natured phone call from a friend can *disturb* someone's rest without *perturbing* the person."

DISUSED/UNUSED (ADJ.)

What is *disused* is no longer used; what is *unused* is not used (a clean glass), new (an *unused* toothbrush), or not used up (*unused* weekly allowance): "The *disused* car was in the backyard next to the *unused* can of gasoline."

DIVIDED/DIVIDING/DIVISIVE (ADJ.)

Anything *divided* contains divisions: "Opinion in our group was *divided:* Some people wanted political change; others didn't."

Things that are *dividing* make divisions: "We hung paintings on the *dividing* wall between the two rooms."

What is *divisive* causes division or disagreement: "The young woman's political remarks were passionate but uncommon and were *divisive* when expressed."

DOMESTICATE/TAME (V.)

To *domesticate* is to accustom an animal to life with people, as in a home or on a farm: "Dogs and pigs have been *domesticated*."

To *tame* an animal is to train it to live among human beings without necessarily removing its wild instincts. People who rescue lion cubs and feed them don't normally keep them around the house as they get bigger, and with good reason: "We need to *tame* the animal before he can be moved to the zoo."

It was Cecil B. DeMille who said, when he made the circus picture *The Greatest Show on Earth*: "You can *tame* a lion, but you can never *domesticate* it."

DOMINATE/DOMINEER/PREDOMINATE (V.)

To *dominate* is to rule or control because of superior power, authority, or strength: "For many years Joe Louis *dominated* heavyweight professional boxing."

To *domineer* is to exercise arbitrary or overbearing tyrannical control: "A tyrant wants to *domineer*." To *domineer* can also mean "to tower over or above": "The castle *domineers* the village."

To *predominate* is to be more important or numerous: "Portuguese *predominates* in Brazil."

DORK/DWEEB (N.)

A *dork* is an unmistakably pejorative term for either a nerd (see GEEK) or a jerk—that is, a stupid, foolish, naive, or obnoxiously unconventional person: "The popular students would call studious, unfashionable kids *dorks*."

The term *dweeb* is used to stigmatize those who are socially inept and considered boring, especially because of extreme studiousness: "Although computer experts can, without self-depreciation, call themselves geeks, they cannot, without self-depreciation, call themselves *dweebs*."

DOUBLE/STAND-IN/UNDERSTUDY (N.)

A *double* is someone who replaces a featured actor when the actor won't be identifiable, as in a crowd or distant shot. The scenes with *doubles* are often shot when the featured actor is busy filming elsewhere or temporarily incapacitated: "The *double* had a build like the actor's."

A *stand-in* is someone who is a substitute for a movie star during the preparation of lighting or cameras or in dangerous scenes: "The *stand-in* was needed for risky chase scenes."

An *understudy* is a reserve actor who knows the featured actor's part well enough to step in for the actor should the actor become ill or otherwise unavailable to complete the part: "The *understudy* was ready to perform when the lead came down with a cold."

DOUBTFUL/DUBIOUS (ADJ.)

Doubtful implies lack of certainty or conviction: "It is *doubtful* whether a third-party candidate will ever, in our day, have a real chance to become president."

Dubious implies a stronger measure of doubt than *doubtful*: "His credentials were *dubious*."

Note that fastidious speakers and writers will often avoid the locution "I am *dubious* about...," preferring "I am *doubtful* about..."

DOWNSTAGE/UPSTAGE (ADV. OR ADJ.)

If you're on the stage of a theater, *downstage* is toward the front of the stage, and *upstage* is toward the rear of the stage: "If you are *downstage*, you're closer to the audience than those who are *upstage*."

DRIZZLE/RAIN (N.)

Drizzle is light precipitation consisting of liquid water drops smaller than *rain* and generally smaller than 0.5 millimeter (0.02 inch) in diameter: "*Drizzle*, normally produced by low stratiform clouds and stratocumulus clouds, largely evaporates before reaching the surface."

Rain consists of drops of water falling to the Earth's surface from clouds: "Although most *rain* reaches the Earth's surface, it is possible in hot, dry desert regions for no *rain* to hit the Earth because of evaporation."

DRONE/WORKER (N.)

A *drone* is a male bee, especially a male honeybee that develops from an unfertilized egg; is larger than the worker; lacks a stinger; takes no part in gathering honey or caring for the hive; and is useful only if a virgin queen requires insemination: "Because *drones* do very little in the world of bees, the word *drone* also applies to lazy human beings who live off others' work."

A *worker* bee is a female honeybee performing such tasks as sealing honey with wax to prevent absorption of moisture from air, feeding *drones*, building honeycombs, and packing pollen into comb cells: "In the summer, about 90 percent of honeybees in a hive are *worker* bees; but in the winter, all bees but the queen are *workers*."

DUCKS/GEESE (N.)

Ducks are smaller than *geese*, often half the size. They are also more slender and have shorter necks than *geese*. While *ducks* are primarily water feeders, most *geese* feed at least as much on land as in water. *Ducks* eat both plants and animals (such as fish and frogs), whereas *geese* are primarily vegetarian, eating pondweeds and grasses. Finally, some *ducks* (the divers rather than the dabblers) go fairly deep under water for their food; *geese* don't dive for food: "If you see dozens of large birds flying together, and you're not sure whether they're *ducks* or *geese*, they are almost certainly *geese* because of their large formation."

DWARF/MIDGET (N.)

Dwarf generally applies to a person having a specific genetic condition, dwarfism, in which the person usually has very short arms and legs and a disproportionately large head: "People are sometimes cruel to *dwarfs* because of their unusually proportioned body parts."

Midget generally applies to an unusually small but well-proportioned person. Adult *midgets* may be thirty inches tall. To many, the term *midget* is offensive; such persons often prefer the expression *little people*: "The *midget*'s body resembled a child's, but his face revealed his age."

E

EACH OTHER/ONE ANOTHER (PRON.)

Each other, in strictest usage, applies to two persons or entities, though that rule often goes unobserved. *One another*, again in strictest usage, applies to three or more persons in reciprocal action or relation. Precise speakers and writers would say, "The two like *each other*," but "It is important for all five of us to respect *one another*."

Nonetheless, neither expression should function as the subject of a verb. Instead of saying "We know how *each other* thinks," say "We each know what the other thinks."

ECHO/REVERBERATION (N.)

An *echo* is the single repetition of a sound caused by the reflection of sound waves from an obstructing surface: "We liked to hear the *echo* of our voices."

When a sound bounces back more than once, it produces a *reverberation*: "The *reverberations* of the man's voice from repeated *echoes* made it difficult to follow what he was saying."

ECLECTIC/FASTIDIOUS/SELECTIVE (ADJ.)

Eclectic necessarily relates to what is borrowed from diverse sources but sometimes means "selecting what appears to be best or true in various doctrines, methods, or styles": "The religious leader had a syncretistic religion, based on an *eclectic* mix of what he believed constituted acceptable doctrines."

Fastidious implies choice involving high and often capricious or excessively demanding standards: "We found it impossible to please the *fastidious* football coach."

Selective implies careful choice: "The university has become increasingly *selective* in its admissions."

EDIFY/EDUCATE (V.)

To *edify* is to instruct and improve, especially in moral and religious wisdom, whereas the word *educate* is a more general word that applies to all skills, instruction, and forms of knowledge. The word *edify* often occurs in the adjectival form *edifying* (enlightening): "The object of reading the encyclopedia is to *educate* oneself; the object of reading the Bible is to be *edified*."

EERIE/UNCANNY/WEIRD (ADJ.)

Something *eerie* produces fear or uneasiness because it is considered strange, mysterious, or supernatural: "Edgar Allan Poe's story 'The Black Cat' is *eerie*."

Uncanny things can arouse feeling because they are inexplicably strange or appear to have a supernatural origin: "At night the deserted house seemed to contain *uncanny* sounds." The word *uncanny* can also refer to a degree so far beyond what is normal or expected as to suggest superhuman or supernatural power: "*Jeopardy!* champion Ken Jennings displayed an *uncanny* ability to quickly recall an enormous range of information."

The word *weird*, the broadest in meaning, can describe what relates to witchcraft or the supernatural but often simply refers to what is odd, strange, or unusual: "Many people think that it is *weird* for a person who has two gloves to wear only one."

EFFECTIVE/EFFECTUAL/EFFICACIOUS/ EFFICIENT (ADJ.)

What is *effective* has the power to produce an effect: "A styptic pencil is *effective* at stopping the bleeding of small shaving cuts."

Effectual activity has accomplished, or can accomplish, a desired result or goal: "After we tried several methods, we discovered which ones were *effectual*."

Efficacious often suggests a strong potential to produce an effect and is often applied to medical remedies or treatments: "Until the discovery of antibiotics and sulfa drugs, there were many diseases for which there were no *efficacious* remedies."

Efficient is to be distinguished from the other terms by meaning "producing a result in a desired or most desirable way": "An *efficient* worker, she would never waste time or supplies."

EFFEMINATE/EFFETE (ADJ.)

Someone is *effeminate* when the person is a male with qualities characteristic of females: "The boys made fun of the man's *effeminate* voice."

What is *effete* is barren, exhausted, or weary. The word originally applied to animals no longer capable of reproducing. It now often applies to something or someone no longer creative: "The authors were productive when they were younger but are now considered *effete*."

E.G./I.E. (ABBR.)

E.g. is an abbreviation for the Latin *exempli grati*, meaning "for example": "Linda had many interests, *e.g.*, swimming, biking, writing, and painting."

The abbreviation *i.e.* is from the Latin *id est*, meaning "that is": "Ray likes root vegetables, *i.e.*, vegetables that grow underground."

EGOIST/EGOTIST (N.)

An *egoist* believes in habitually looking out for number one: "We regarded most politicians as *egoists*, pretending to put others' interests ahead of their own."

An *egotist* is a conceited, boastful person: "The *egotist* claimed to be the greatest radio personality of his generation."

ÉLAN/VERVE (N.)

Élan refers to vigor, spirit, or enthusiasm, especially as revealed by a brilliant and self-confident performance: "At his best, Michael Jordan played basketball with an *élan* that few people can even come close to matching."

Verve refers to a lively and forceful quality or manner of composition or performance, often describing paintings and musical works: "Yo Yo Ma plays the cello with extraordinary technical proficiency and *verve*."

ELECTRIC/ELECTRONIC (ADJ.)

Electric means "of, relating to, or operated by electricity": "I have an *electric* lamp, *electric* toaster, and *electric* stove."

Electronic describes (1) equipment, such as televisions and computers, whose current is controlled by transistors, valves, and similar components, or (2) the components themselves: "A digital watch is *electronic*, though it works with electricity from a small battery."

ELEMENTAL/ELEMENTARY (ADJ.)

Elemental means "relating to, or caused by, a great force of nature," "comparable (especially in power) to a force or object of nature," or "relating to a chemical element": "On the sailboat, we were impressed by the *elemental* force of the ocean."

Elementary means "introductory," "rudimentary," or "fundamental": "Before one progresses to advanced math, one must master *elementary* arithmetic."

ELUDE/EVADE (V.)

Elude comes closer to "escape" than to "avoid," but often suggests a slippery or baffling quality in the thing that gets away: "The answer to the puzzle *eludes* us." When people *elude* others, they usually do it slyly or adroitly but not necessarily dishonestly: "The beautiful woman tried to *elude* strangers who seemed overeager to initiate conversation."

To *evade* is to get away from (a pursuer, an enemy, or even a lawful authority) by dexterity or strategy. The word often suggests trying to get away with some action while avoiding disagreeable consequences for oneself, especially by underhanded or even illegitimate means: "The criminal tried to *evade* the police."

EMPATHY/SYMPATHY (N.)

Empathy is the ability to imagine oneself in another person's position and to experience all the thoughts, feelings, and sensations connected with it: "Her *empathy* prompts her to share in the embarrassment when she encounters someone who feels embarrassed."

Sympathy is compassion for or commiseration with another: "We sent him a card to express our *sympathy* for the loss of his father."

EMPEROR/KING/MONARCH/ SOVEREIGN (N.)

An *emperor* is the supreme ruler of an empire: "The *emperor* of Japan during World War II was Hirohito."

A *king* or queen is the hereditary head of a kingdom, state, or nation: "*King* George III was a stubborn man who wouldn't accede to the demands of the American colonists."

A *monarch* or a *sovereign* is a king, queen, emperor, or empress. A *monarch* can rule a limited or absolute monarchy, depending on whether the ruler has constitutional limitations: "King Louis XIV was an absolute *monarch*; Queen Elizabeth II is a limited *monarch*." "The *sovereign* claimed that he was not bound by law but was its creator."

EMULATE/IMITATE (V.)

To *emulate* implies a conscious effort to equal or surpass someone or something by imitation or by using the person or thing as an inspiring model: "Children are fortunate when they find extraordinary people they want to *emulate*."

To *imitate* is simply to copy: "A person may become a competent pianist by *imitating* good pianists, but great pianists need to develop their own style."

ENDEMIC/EPIDEMIC/PANDEMIC (ADJ./N.)

Endemic, *epidemic*, and *pandemic* all describe the occurrence of a disease in a population.

An *endemic* disease constantly exists to some extent in a certain population or region: "Malaria has been *endemic* in Liberia."

An *epidemic* disease breaks out, rages in a community beyond expectations, and later subsides: "In some communities, cholera became *epidemic* that year."

A *pandemic* disease occurs over a wide area and affects an exceptionally large proportion of the population: "Malaria was *pandemic* in that region until the introduction of quinine."

ENORMITY/ENORMOUSNESS (N.)

Enormity designates the quality or state of exceeding a measure or rule, or being immoderate, monstrous, or outrageous. Although *enormity* can be a synonym for *hugeness* or *immensity*, it is less confusing to use those words and reserve *enormity* for something that is somehow excessive or monstrous: "We had trouble believing the *enormity* of Hitler's crimes."

Enormousness is a neutral term designating hugeness or immensity: "It is difficult to imagine the *enormousness* of one galaxy, much less the *enormousness* of the universe."

ENVY/JEALOUSY (N.)

Envy describes a painful or resentful awareness of an advantage enjoyed by another, accompanied by a desire for the same advantage: "We thought the woman's wealth attracted much *envy*."

Although *jealous* can describe zealous vigilance (a *jealous* protection of one's honor or people's rights), it more usually describes a state of distrustful, suspicious, angry, or discontented intolerance of the possibility of someone's coming to possess what is regarded as belonging to or befitting oneself: "The *jealous* man was incensed whenever another man ogled his wife."

Normally, one experiences *envy* of what one wants to have and *jealousy* of what one fears losing.

ÉPÉE/FOIL (N.)

An *épée* is a fencing or dueling sword having a bowl-shaped guard (to protect the hand), a rigid thirty-five-inch blade with no cutting edge, and a blunted point at the end of the blade: "In a pirate movie, some actors need to learn to fence with *épées*."

A *foil* is a fencing weapon resembling an *épée* but weighing less and having a flat guard and a more flexible blade: "The boy learning fencing preferred the *foil* to the *épée* because it weighed less."

EQUABLE/EQUITABLE (ADJ.)

What is *equable* is steady, uniform, or not easily upset: "Always the *equable* woman, Mary kept her composure even when others around her lost theirs."

What is *equitable* is fair and equal to all concerned: "We thought that the distribution of his inheritance to the beneficiaries was *equitable*."

ERROR/MISTAKE (N.)

An *error* is an incorrect belief, judgment, perception, or conclusion, or an ignorant or imprudent deviation from a code of behavior: "Jason made six *errors* on the test."

A *mistake* suggests a misunderstanding, a wrong decision, or an inadvertent wrong action. *Mistakes* are often unimportant, but they can sometimes have serious consequences: "If a student writes the equation 2 + 2 = 1,000,286, that sum is too big to be a *mistake*."

EVASION/EVASIVENESS (N.)

Evasion designates a physical escape or flight or an act of evading, dodging, or equivocating: "The politician's response to the question was not a real answer but an *evasion*."

Whereas *evasion* is something one does, *evasiveness* is an attribute one possesses, a temperament: "We didn't appreciate their *evasiveness* in answering our question."

EXALT/EXTOL/EXULT (V.)

Exalt means "to raise high (in rank, dignity, or power)" or "to glorify or elevate by praise or in estimation": "My father *exalted* personal responsibility over all other virtues."

Extol is to praise highly or eulogize: "Politicians who *extol* limited government rarely approve of legislation that weakens the government's power or authority."

Exult means "to be extremely joyful" or "to be elated or delighted": "The winner of the contest *exulted* over having won two hundred thousand dollars."

EXAMINE/INSPECT/INVESTIGATE (V.)

Examine usually suggests a detailed questioning or scrutiny to determine condition or quality: "The coroner *examined* the body for cause of death."

Inspect suggests a careful search for flaws, errors, or violations: "Those in quality control must *inspect* products or services."

Investigate suggests systematic probing, inquiry, or search: "The personnel from the crime lab *investigated* the evidence."

EXCEED/EXCEL (V.)

To *exceed* is to be greater than or to go beyond the limits of: "She wanted to *exceed* the speed limit."

To *excel* is to be better than or superior to: "If people *excel* at the piano, they play it better than most people do."

EXCEPT/EXEMPT (V.)

What is *excepted* is not included: "All the wine *except* one bottle was expensive."

To *exempt* is to exclude from some requirement: "In certain contexts, members of the military may be *exempted* from paying federal income tax."

EXCITE/INCITE (V.)

To *excite* is to stimulate or move profoundly: "The rock performer *excited* the crowd with her stirring music."

To *incite* is to stir up and urge on, often by actively prompting: "The paid agitators *incited* the riot."

EXCORIATE/EXECRATE (V.)

To *excoriate* means literally "to strip or wear off the skin of" and figuratively "to censure scathingly": "Bob's boss *excoriated* him for endangering his coworkers."

To *execrate* is to denounce, curse, or abhor: "The man was *execrated* as a vicious murderer."

EXPEDIENT/EXPEDITIOUS (ADJ.)

What is *expedient* is advantageous or suitable to the circumstances, or advisable on political or practical grounds but not on moral grounds: "We should prefer just action to *expedient* action when the two conflict."

What is *expeditious* is suitable for and done with speed and efficiency: "We complimented the courier for *expeditious* service."

EXPLICIT/EXPRESS (ADJ.)

Both *explicit* and *express* describe unmistakably clear actions or statements.

Anything *explicit* is so clear and distinct that there is nothing left to be inferred or to be misinterpreted by being vague or ambiguous: "The violence in Hitchcock's movies is usually suggested rather than *explicit*."

Anything *expressed* is uttered with directness, pointedness, or force: "The witness's *express* testimony proved decisive in convicting the defendant."

EXPRESSWAY/FREEWAY/PARKWAY/ THRUWAY/TURNPIKE (N.)

In the United States, an *expressway* is a divided highway with a limited number of at-grade intersections (where roads or roads and railways can cross), making it a form of high-speed arterial road: "The *expressway* allowed for fast traffic except at its few intersections."

A *freeway* is a multiple-lane highway designed for safer high-speed operation of motor vehicles by eliminating cross traffic. *Freeways* have controlled access at interchanges or junctions, where traffic can move from one highway to another with crossing traffic: "We loved using the *freeway* because we enjoyed not having to stop for traffic lights."

A *parkway* is a divided road that is a broad landscaped thoroughfare, especially one from which trucks and other heavy vehicles are excluded: "We loved using the *parkway* because of the attractive trees."

A *thruway* is a highway for which access is limited to well-spaced intervals: "Because we weren't in a hurry and didn't want to stop for intersecting traffic, we took the *thruway*."

A *turnpike* often has three lanes but is distinguished by requiring a toll: "The New Jersey *Turnpike* is one of the most famous roads in America."

EXTEMPORANEOUS/IMPROMPTU (ADJ.)

Although both *extemporaneous* and *impromptu* are often used to describe actions performed at the spur of the moment, an *extemporaneous* speech is traditionally one that is carefully prepared but delivered without notes or text, whereas an *impromptu* speech is made up or improvised on the spot: "We are impressed by *extemporaneous* speeches but are impressed even more by *impromptu* ones."

EXTRACT/EXTRICATE (V.)

To *extract* implies the use of force or pressure in obtaining what is to be *extracted*, whether a tooth or information: "We were able to *extract* the information from the witness, but only after much effort."

To *extricate* usually implies using care or ingenuity in freeing someone or something from a difficult position or situation or disentangling what is *extricated*: "We'll need to be highly resourceful to *extricate* the hostages from their captors."

F

FABLE/TALE (N.)

A *fable* is a brief *tale*, in prose or verse, to illustrate a moral. Often involving unusual or supernatural incidents, *fables* sometimes contain animals, as in *Aesop's Fables*, Rudyard Kipling's *The Jungle Book*, and George Orwell's *Animal Farm*: "The *fables* of Aesop illustrate important morals."

In literature, a *tale* is simply a recital of a series of events, in prose or verse. A *tale* can be any recitation of events, whether fiction or nonfiction: "We let the child tell us his *tale* of woe."

FACILITY/FACULTY (N.)

Facility is ease or dexterity or something that promotes the ease of any action, operation, or transaction (excellent *facilities* for legal studies): "We were impressed by the *facility* with which the virtuoso played the piano."

A *faculty*, as distinguished from *facility*, is an ability to act or do, whether inborn or acquired: "His *faculty* for mathematics made him an excellent accountant."

FACTITIOUS/FICTITIOUS (ADJ.)

What is *factitious* is artificially engineered or manufactured, including anything not occurring spontaneously or naturally: "The applause of the employees was as *factitious* as the flowers in the lobby."

What is *fictitious* is invented, untrue, or not genuine: "We discovered that his story about his past was *fictitious*."

FAKE/FRAUD (N.)

A *fake* is any person or thing not genuine: "His watch looked like a Rolex, but it was a *fake*."

A *fraud* is either a person who is not what he or she pretends to be or a deliberate deception to try to cheat people out of something of value: "The con man perpetrated a *fraud*, cheating some people out of thousands of dollars."

FAMILIARITY/INTIMACY (N.)

Familiarity suggests an informal closeness: "They needed to have a *familiarity* with geography to do well on the test."

Intimacy suggests very close association, possibly private and personal. "Her love letters reflected an *intimacy* too personal to be published."

FAMISHED/RAVENOUS/RAVISHED (ADJ.)

To be *famished* is to be intensely hungry or to lack necessities: "We were happy to get food to the *famished* people."

Ravenous implies excessive hunger and suggests violent or grasping methods of dealing with food and with whatever satisfies an appetite: "Hitler had a *ravenous* lust for power."

Ravished describes being seized and violently carried away or sexually violated, or transported with joy or delight: "The young man was *ravished* by his date's beauty."

FARTHER/FURTHER (ADV./ADJ.)

Farther and *further* can both describe anything at or to a greater or more advanced point, or to a greater degree or extent. As adverbs, they are often used interchangeably whenever spatial, temporal, or figurative distance is involved: "The two walked *farther* [*further*]." Nonetheless, careful speakers and writers prefer *farther* for physical distance (as in the example sentence just given) and *further* for figurative distance, as follows: "We traveled *farther* before running into *further* problems."

FATIGUED/TIRED/WEARY (ADJ.)

Fatigue is weariness from labor or exertion; a *fatigued* person suffers from mental or physical exhaustion: "Working two days without sleeping *fatigued* her."

To be *tired* is to be drained of one's strength and patience: "The boy was so *tired* that he had trouble paying attention to his teacher's instructions."

To be *weary* can describe being exhausted in strength, freshness, or endurance but often implies having one's interest, patience, or indulgence worn out: "We grew *weary* from repeatedly hearing the same anecdote."

FECUND/FERTILE (ADJ.)

Fecund stresses abundance or rapidity of reproduction: "From da Vinci's *fecund* imagination came many inventions."

Fertile refers simply to the ability to reproduce: "Because the woman was *fertile* and wanted to have children, she decided to start her family."

FERMENT/FOMENT (V.)

To the extent that the two words should be distinguished, *ferment* means "to excite, to stir up, or to agitate": "The increasing popularity of a belief in democratic rule *fermented* many governments in the eighteenth and nineteenth centuries."

Foment indicates persistent inciting, especially of something viewed as seething or boiling. *Foment* often implies urging or stimulating into action, especially in an unfavorable context: "The activists wanted to *foment* a riot."

FERVENT/FERVID (ADJ.)

A *fervent* desire suggests the quality of fire, but a fire that glows rather than bursts into flame. It suggests heat, but heat that is deep, steady, and sustained. It is especially applied to wishes, prayers, or hopes, particularly when they are deep and heartfelt: "Nothing can shake her *fervent* loyalty to her cause."

Fervid applies more to moods and expressions than to persons, often suggesting obvious, warmly expressed, and spontaneous emotion: "Karen's *fervid* embrace of her boyfriend offended a reserved onlooker."

FETTER/MANACLE (N.)

Fetters are shackles (or metal restraints) for the feet: "The chain gang wore *fetters*, so they had to move together and in the same direction."

Manacles are shackles for the hands or wrists that are usually heavier than handcuffs: "We were instructed to put *manacles* on the prisoner's wrists once his hands were behind his back."

FEUD/VENDETTA (N.)

A *feud* is a bitter, protracted, and sometimes violent quarrel or hostility between individuals or factions: "The *feud* between the Hatfields and the McCoys turned deadly."

A *vendetta* (Italian via the Latin *vindicta* for "vengeance") is a long and violent *feud* in which one side harms the other in retaliation for previous harms: "The *vendetta* between the warring crime families led to a series of retaliatory homicides."

FEWER (ADJ.)/LESS (ADJ. AND ADV.)

Fewer refers to countable things: "That line is for ten items or *fewer*."

Less is comparative and refers to matters of degree: "She expressed *less* enthusiasm than we expected."

FIANCÉ/FIANCÉE (N.)

Fiancé is the man who is engaged to be married; *fiancée*, the woman: "Bob was Rachel's *fiancé*, and Rachel was Bob's *fiancée*."

FIELD/MEADOW (N.)

A *field* is any open expanse of level land: "Beaver and Wally Cleaver like to play in Metzger's *Field*."

A *meadow* is land in or predominantly in grass, either in its natural state or used as pasture for growing hay: "The *meadow* was low, flat, and near a river."

FILM/MOVIE (N.)

Both *film* and *movie* can refer to the same thing, but connotatively the term *film* is more often used to suggest that the director has something to say and isn't out "simply" to entertain: "The *film Network*, unlike the *movie Meatballs*, contains powerful drama and social commentary as well as humor."

FIRING/LAYOFF/POSITION ELIMINATION/ TERMINATION (N.)

Firing usually designates for-cause dismissal, as for employee theft, gross insubordination, or release of proprietary information: "Stephanie was *fired* for stealing clothes from where she worked."

Layoff usually designates dismissing hourly employees "subject to recall": "The *layoff* of hourly workers was due to the recession."

Position elimination designates permanent elimination of a job, usually as a result of workforce reduction, plant closings, or departmental consolidations: "Many workers lost jobs at several Virginia governmental agencies because of *position elimination*."

Termination often designates dismissing workers

because of unsatisfactory performance: "John's constant tardiness resulted in his *termination*."

FISCAL/MONETARY (ADJ.)

Fiscal relates to administering financial affairs (debts, taxes, revenues, and expenditures) of a public or private organization: "Some critics say that America's huge federal debt is a product of *fiscal* irresponsibility."

Monetary relates to actual money and its supply: "Many economists argue that the Great Depression was exacerbated by a *monetary* policy in which the supply of money was excessively restricted."

FLAIR/FLARE (N.)

A *flair* is a natural ability, capacity, instinct, or bent: "Her *flair* for hospitality endeared her to many people."

A *flare* is an unsteady glaring light or a sudden outburst, as of sound, excitement, or anger: "He apologized for his *flare* of temper."

FLAT/LEVEL (ADJ.)

A *flat* surface is smooth, even, uncured, and on one plane: "A *flat* surface can be horizontal or vertical or somewhere between."

A *level* surface is one parallel to the horizon: "A wall is *flat* without being *level*."

FLEECE/FUR (N.)

A *fleece* is the coat of wool from a sheep: "Mary's lamb had a *fleece* as white as snow."

Fur applies to the hairy coat of a mammal or an article of clothing made from the coat: "Polar bears need a heavy coat of *fur* to insulate them from the cold."

FLINCH/WINCE (V.)

To *flinch* is to withdraw or shrink (as from a challenge or responsibility), usually because of the danger, difficulties, or distress involved: "She never *flinched* from her responsibilities."

To *wince* is to shrink back involuntarily, as from pain or fear. The word is normally used to describe pulling a face in pain—or as if in pain—and is used figuratively to mean "felt the pain of embarrassment": "His crude jokes made modest people *wince*."

FLOTSAM/JETSAM/LAGAN (N.)

Flotsam is the floating cargo or wreckage of a ship. The word is related in meaning and origin to *float*: "We saw some luggage in the *flotsam*."

Jetsam describes any cargo or equipment jettisoned aboard during a storm or an emergency: "We got rid of the *jetsam* to lighten our load during the storm."

Lagan describes any goods jettisoned and tied to a buoy to aid recovery: "The buoys attached to the floating material indicated *lagan*."

FLOUNDER/FOUNDER (V.)

To *flounder* is to struggle awkwardly or thrash about, or to struggle or stumble helplessly to try to make progress: "We suggested tutors for the students who began to *flounder*."

To *founder* is to become disabled or to sink: "Unless

they repaired the damage to the hull of the boat, they would *founder.*"

FOAM/FROTH/SUDS (N.)

Foam is a collection of tiny bubbles forming on the surface of a liquid for various reasons, such as by shaking or fermentation: "We noticed the thick *foam* on the head of the beer."

Froth is like *foam*, but it has larger bubbles that are more evanescent than those of *foam.* Consequently, things that are light or ephemeral are called *froth*, not *foam*: "Before the man passed out, we noticed *froth* on his lips."

Suds are *foam* or *froth* on the surface of soapy water, or a synonym for beer because of its sudsy head: "The fraternity members liked to drink *suds.*"

FOOLHARDY/FOOLISH (ADJ.)

People are *foolhardy* when they foolishly expose themselves to danger: "It was *foolhardy* for the boy to walk down the dark alley alone and intoxicated."

People are *foolish* if they are unable to use judgment, discretion, or good sense: "Those students are *foolish* if they think they can earn excellent grades at a demanding university without ever studying."

FORCEFUL/FORCIBLE (ADJ.)

Forceful means "having great force"; *forcible* means "using force": "The man in the audience who brandished a gun during the politician's *forceful* speech was *forcibly* removed."

FOREST/WOODS (N.)

Both *forest* and *woods* describe a dense growth of trees and underbrush. *Woods* describes a dense growth of trees usually greater than that of a grove but smaller than that of a *forest*: "People are more likely to become lost in a *forest* than in a *woods*."

FOREWORD/INTRODUCTION/PREFACE (N.)

A *foreword* is a discussion of the book by someone other than the author, often a celebrity or noted expert. The discussion will usually explain why the book should be read: "The prolific author Isaac Asimov wrote many *forewords*."

An *introduction* is often a long discussion by the author about the subject of the book. It is like a movie preview, luring readers to the main attraction: "The author's *introduction* revealed the author's attitude toward the subject of the book."

A *preface* is a short discussion by the author about the purpose, background, and structure of the book: "The *preface* explained why the author wrote the book."

FORT/FORTRESS (N.)

A *fort* is a military installation fortified with troops, weapons, and barricades. A *fortress* is larger than a *fort*. Further, the word, when used in contradistinction to *fort*, describes a large, permanent military stronghold, sometimes including a town: "In the American West, *forts* were often simply log palisades with blockhouses at the corners and were not as big or impressive as *fortresses*."

FORTUITOUS/FORTUNATE (ADJ.)

A *fortuitous* event occurs by luck or chance, whether *fortunate*, unfortunate, or neutral: "My arriving at the restaurant during the special bargain was not planned but *fortuitous*."

A *fortunate* event reflects good fortune or favorable luck: "I was *fortunate* to win five hundred thousand dollars on the TV quiz show."

FOYER/LOBBY (N.)

A *foyer* can be an entranceway or transitional area from the exterior of a building to its interior: "We entered a *foyer* before entering the *lobby*."

A *lobby* is a space inside the entrance to a building, theater, or auditorium: "We waited for our cab in the hotel *lobby*."

FRANKFURTER/HOT DOG (N.)

A *frankfurter* becomes a *hot dog* when the sausage is placed in a roll. Although many people use the expression *hot dog* to designate a *frankfurter*, a person who ate three *hot dogs* for lunch is presumed to have also eaten three rolls—unless we're informed otherwise: "I bought six *frankfurters* and then bought a package of rolls to make the *hot dogs*."

FRESCO/MURAL (N.)

A *fresco* is a painting done on freshly spread moist lime plaster with water-based pigments—that is, a wall (or ceiling) painting done while the plaster is still damp: "Michelangelo's *frescoes* in the Sistine Chapel have survived more than four centuries."

A *mural* is artwork executed on a wall or occasionally on a ceiling. Leonardo da Vinci's painting *The Last Supper* was a *mural*: "Because *The Last Supper* was created as an oil *mural* on a damp wall, the paint began to peel not long after Leonardo's death."

FRIAR/MONK (N.)

A *friar* is a member of a certain religious order of men, especially the four mendicant orders (Augustinians, Carmelites, Dominicans, and Franciscans), originally relying only on alms: "The *friar* belonged to the Dominicans."

A *monk* is a man belonging to a religious community (monastery) typically living under vows of poverty, chastity, and obedience: "A man who enjoys eating, drinking, and female companionship is probably ill suited to become a *monk*."

FROG/TOAD (N.)

Although both *frogs* and *toads* are tailless amphibians, they differ in at least four obvious respects. *Frogs* like water, are smooth skinned, leap, and have teeth. *Toads*, except when breeding, aren't aquatic; are dry, rough skinned, and warty (though they don't cause warts); and are toothless: "When we saw tooth marks on the little girl, we reasoned that she had been bitten by a *frog* because tooth marks can't come from *toads*."

FROWN/SCOWL (N.)

A *frown* commonly implies a stern face and contracted brows, expressing displeasure, disapproval, anger, or contempt: "When the pupil was called down for his prank, his smile quickly turned into a *frown*."

A *scowl* often implies a wrinkled drawn-down brow expressing ill humor, sullenness, or discontent: "A *scowl* often describes a look that may be gloomy and threatening, whereas a *frown* is normally not closely associated with a threatening look."

FRUGAL/THRIFTY (ADJ.)

Both *frugal* and *thrifty* emphasize saving or making unwasteful use of money, goods, or resources.

Frugal implies not only simplicity and temperance but also abstention from all luxury: "A *frugal* man, he would never buy a luxury car."

Thrifty implies minimizing wastefulness and maximizing saving, usually reflecting industry: "Miserly people hoard money out of avarice, whereas *thrifty* people save money out of prudence."

G

GARGANTUAN/GIGANTIC (ADJ.)

Gargantua is the fictional name of Rabelais's giant, who has a *gargantuan* appetite. Consequently, *gargantuan* is best applied to quantities of food and drink, as in *gargantuan* helpings, portions, or thirst: "The football player had a *gargantuan* appetite."

The word *gigantic* (huge) is more flexible and, unlike *gargantuan*, can modify things that have nothing to do with physical appetites: "We realize that the experiment was a *gigantic* failure."

GARISH/GAUDY (ADJ.)

Both *garish* and *gaudy* can describe what is showy, including loud colors or excessive ornamentation. *Gaudy* reflects a greater lack of taste than *garish* does: "The woman was able to wear her *garish* watch without hearing many negative comments, but she wasn't equally fortunate when she wore her *gaudy* shocking pink dress."

GEEK/NERD (N.)

A *geek* is any intelligent person with an obsessive interest, as in computers, science fiction, comic books, politics, or even sports. Although the term has often been pejorative, it can be used almost neutrally or sometimes even positively, as when computer experts proudly call themselves *geeks*: "Whenever we had computer trouble, we paged the brightest *geek* in the office."

A *nerd* is a socially inept or awkward and often unstylish *geek*. Often gravitating toward math, science, and technology, *nerds* are known for their scholastic drive and may be comfortable with themselves yet are often uncomfortable in demanding social situations, such as parties: "Though highly intelligent, the *nerd* was visibly uncomfortable at parties."

GEM/JEWEL (N.)

A *gem* is a precious or semiprecious stone that has been cut and polished to serve as an ornament. "The *gem* in his ring caught my eye."

A *jewel* can describe either a precious stone or a precious metal (especially gold, silver, or platinum) often set with stone as an accessory of dress: "The *jewel* the woman wore was set with precious stones."

GENOCIDE/MASSACRE/POGROM/ SLAUGHTER (N.)

Genocide, *massacre*, *pogrom*, and *slaughter* can all describe a great and often wanton killing of human beings.

Genocide is the systematic and planned extermination of an entire national, racial, political, or ethnic group: "Both Stalin and Hitler ordered the *genocide* of millions of people."

Massacre implies indiscriminate and wholesale killing, especially of those unable to defend themselves and incapable of making much or any resistance: "The men killed women and children in the *massacre* of the tribe."

Pogrom applies especially to an organized *massacre* of helpless people, usually with the connivance of officials. The term often applies to the *massacre* of European Jews: "In 1903, there were several *pogroms* of Russian Jews."

Slaughter, a butcher's term for killing animals for food, suggests extensive and ruthless killing, whether in a battle or a *massacre*: "The soldiers seemed to enjoy the *slaughter* of the villagers."

GESTICULATE/GESTURE (V.)

Although the two words can sometimes be used interchangeably, *gesticulate* refers to the act of making *gestures* (especially with the hands or arms), and *gesture* is the motion itself. *Gesture* is the preferred word for describing simple motions: "We *gestured* for a cab." "Mary was excitedly *gesticulating* with her hands as she expressed her complaint."

GHERKIN/PICKLE (N.)

A *gherkin* is the immature fruit of the cucumber, especially when it is used for pickling, whereas a *pickle* is a *gherkin* that has been preserved in brine or vinegar—in short, pickled: "She enjoyed *gherkins*, but only before they became *pickles*."

GHOST/PHANTOM/SPECTER (N.)

A *ghost* is a disembodied soul or spirit of a dead person, sometimes thought to appear to the living in pale bodily likeness: "We were told that the house was haunted by a *ghost*."

A *phantom* is something that appears to be seen, heard, or sensed but has no actual or substantial existence: "The vision appeared to be a *phantom* because we seemed to walk through it."

A *specter* can be a *ghost*, especially if it is frightening or terrifying. The word is often used figuratively to describe anything that inspires fear or dread: "The political revolution raised the *specter* of economic collapse."

GIBE/JIBE (V.)

To *gibe* is to offer taunting sarcastic words, when the verb has no object: "The boys *gibed* at Tom for his accent." To *gibe* people is to sneer at them: "They *gibed* each other for eccentricities."

To *jibe* is to match or agree with: "The accounts of the two witnesses don't *jibe*."

GLANCE/GLIMPSE (V.)

A *glance* is a quick, brief, hurried, or cursory look: "The girls were flattered by the boys' darting *glances*."

A *glimpse* is a fleeting and normally incomplete view: "Because the movie star jogged past us, we got only a *glimpse* of her face."

GLARE/GLOWER (N.)

A *glare* is a look expressing intense hostility, annoyance, or dislike, or an angry, intense stare: "The accused gave the district attorney a threatening *glare*."

A *glower* is a sullen, brooding, angry look, often

suggesting gloominess: "His *glower* revealed that he was both angry and sullen."

GLEAM/GLIMMER (N.)

A *gleam* is either a fleeting flash of light or a fleeting appearance of something seen through an intervening medium or from a distance: "We like to get up early to see the *gleam* of dawn."

A *glimmer* is a feeble or intermittent light, a dim perception, or a vague manifestation: "His insensitive remarks at the party revealed a *glimmer* of his personality."

GLOSS/LUSTER/SHEEN (N.)

Gloss is a superficial glowing *luster*: "We immediately noticed the *gloss* of her satin dress."

Luster is the glow of reflected light: "The pearl had a beautiful *luster*."

Sheen is a glistening brightness, a soft *luster*, especially the shininess given to textiles: "She liked the *sheen* of the rayon sweater."

GLUE/PASTE (N.)

Glue is protein gelatin, formed by boiling animal hides or bones in water: "The old joke about riding horses to the *glue* factory has a historical basis."

Paste can be produced by a simple mixture of water, flour, and starch: "She preferred to use *paste* because it didn't require the use of dead animals."

GOURMAND/GOURMET (N.)

A *gourmand* likes to eat well and heartily and tends to be gluttonous: "The *gourmand* loved to go to all-you-can-eat buffets."

A *gourmet* is a connoisseur of food and drink but needn't be at all gluttonous: "The *gourmet* regularly enjoyed fine wine."

GRADATION/NUANCE/SHADE (N.)

Gradation, when used in the singular, describes a small difference or variation. More often the word occurs in the plural, in which usage it usually signifies the successive steps by which a thing passes from a thing of one kind to a thing of another kind: "The intermediate colors by which blue gradually passes into green are *gradations*."

Nuance signifies a subtle or slight degree of difference, as in meaning, feeling, tone, or tint: "An aim of *The Artful Nuance* is to reveal the *nuances* between words of related meaning."

Shade implies a minute or barely perceptible degree of difference, as in thought, belief, or position: "Every *shade* of political opinion was represented at the convention."

GRAMMAR/SYNTAX (N.)

Grammar is the linguistic study dealing with the classes of words and their relationships to one another, as indicated in inflections, spelling, pronunciation, etymology, and semantics: "In studying *grammar*, we learned the parts of speech."

Syntax is the part of *grammar* that is especially concerned with the arrangement of word forms to show their mutual relations in sentences: "If people understand English *syntax*, they'll understand that word order can substantially affect the meaning of sentences."

GRAVE/TOMB (N.)

A *grave* is a cavity in the earth; a *tomb* can be a *grave*, a crypt, or a vault that is wholly or partly in the earth or entirely above ground: "The peasant was buried in a shallow *grave*, but the king was buried in a large, ornate *tomb* with pillars at the entrance."

GRIEVE/MOURN (V.)

To *grieve* is to feel deep sorrow because of loss or distress: "We knew that she would *grieve* over her ex-husband's death."

To *mourn* usually implies the demonstration of grief, especially over a death: "The sadness on her face showed that she was *mourning* her friend's death."

GRILL/GRILLE (N.)

A *grill* is a cooking grate or surface: "We bought charcoal for the *grill*."

A *grille* is a grating (as of iron, bronze, or wood) designed to serve as a barrier or decoration: "We were impressed by the elaborate *grille* on the outer door."

GRISLY/GRISTLY/GRIZZLED/GRIZZLY (ADJ.)

Anything *grisly* inspires horror or intense fear: "As a soldier, the man had seen many *grisly* things."

Gristly means "full of gristle": "The steak was too *gristly* for me to enjoy."

Grizzled means "grayish": "We noticed the man's *grizzled* beard."

Grizzly is a type of bear and a word meaning "grayish" or "flecked with gray," related to *grizzled*: "They were frightened by the *grizzly* bear."

GROAN/MOAN (N.)

A *groan* is usually a deep, fairly loud, and mostly brief sound: "The boxer fell with a *groan*."

A *moan* is generally a soft, long, and possibly high-pitched sound: "The soldier said he'd never forget the *moans* of those wounded in battle."

H

HARBINGER/HERALD (N.)

A *harbinger* can be a person or thing that is a sign of something to come: "The crocus is a *harbinger* of spring."

A *herald* can literally be an official messenger, especially one carrying or proclaiming important news, as from royal personages. Because *herald* can be used to refer to a sign or an indication of something to come, it can overlap in meaning with *harbinger*, though *harbinger* appears to be more common in the sense of an omen: "The king had a *herald* who announced his arrival."

HARBOR/PORT (N.)

Harbor designates a part of a body of water (as a sea or lake) partially or almost totally enclosed, which can protect entering ships or boats when they are moored: "The ship was safe once it was moored in the *harbor*."

Port designates a place, usually both a *harbor* and an adjacent city or town, suitable for landing people or goods: "The steamers docked in the *port* of New York."

HARI-KIRI/KAMIKAZE (N.)

Both *hari-kiri* and *kamikaze* refer to Japanese suicide. *Hari-kiri* is suicide by disembowelment (slitting the belly), formerly practiced by the Japanese samurai or decreed to a member by a feudal court in lieu of the ordinary death penalty: "John Belushi, on *Saturday Night Live*, used to portray a samurai who would prepare for *hari-kiri* whenever people were displeased with him."

Kamikaze (Japanese for "divine wind") designates either a member of the Japanese air attack corp assigned to crash into enemy ships or an airplane containing explosives for a suicidal crash: "The *kamikazes* saw themselves as fulfilling their religious and patriotic ideals."

HAY/STRAW (N.)

Hay, composed of dried grasses, oats, alfalfa, or barley, is food for cattle and horses: "We feed *hay* to the horses."

Straw consists of dried stalks of grain that are mixed with leaves and chaff. *Straw* is used as bedding for cattle, packing, papermaking, and so on: "The animal slept on a bed of *straw*."

HEALTHFUL/HEALTHY (ADJ.)

What is *healthful* promotes health; what is *healthy* enjoys good health: "The *healthy* woman ate *healthful* food."

HEATHEN/INFIDEL/PAGAN (N.)

A *heathen* was originally any polytheist, including adherents of the idol-worshiping faiths of ancient Egypt, Greece, and Rome. During the Middle Ages, the term came to designate anyone who didn't acknowledge what was regarded as the one and true God: "Mono-theists, including Jews, Christians, and Muslims, have used *heathen* to describe anyone not accepting their religion."

An *infidel*, from the Latin *infidelus* ("unfaithful"), is a *heathen* who doesn't believe in the prevailing religion of the land: "Muslims living in Muslim-dominated lands during the Crusades called Christians *infidels*, and the Christians called Muslims *heathens*."

A *pagan* can designate a follower of ancient Greek or Roman religion or any *heathen* worshiping Earth gods through roots, stones, and water: "The Druids of the ancient Celts and Gauls are examples of *pagans*."

HERB/SPICE (N.)

Herbs are obtained from the leaves of herbaceous (nonwoody) plants. Many are used to add flavor when cooking, and some have medicinal value. They are often used in larger amounts than *spices*, which are often more potent. The word *herbs* can be used also in a strict botanical sense to denote any nonwoody plants that die at the end of the growing season, regardless of their usefulness to people. Some *herbs* can, however, survive the winter, especially if they are grown in fairly mild climates or if they are protected, as by a layer of snow: "She added the *herbs* thyme and sage to her soup."

Spices are obtained from roots, flowers, fruits, seeds, or bark (for example, cinnamon). They are native to warm tropical climates and can be woody plants. Because *spices* are often stronger and more potent than *herbs*, they are typically used in smaller amounts. The word *spice* can also describe aromatic and pungent condiments made from vegetables: "He decided to give the recipe more flavor by adding *spices* like cinnamon and nutmeg."

HERNIA/RUPTURE (N.)

A *hernia* is the protrusion or projection of an organ through an abnormal opening in the wall of the cavity containing the organ: "A bulge in the groin can be an inguinal *hernia*."

A *rupture* is any tear or break, including the tearing apart by force, disease, or some other cause in an organ or structure: "There was a *rupture* in his heart."

HIDE/PELT (N.)

A *hide* is the skin of a large animal, such as a buffalo, deer, or lion. A *pelt* is the skin of a smaller animal, such as a fox, rabbit, or mink: "His belt was made of cow-*hide*, and his wife's stole came from a mink *pelt*."

HISTORIC/HISTORICAL (ADJ.)

While *historic* means "famous or important in history," *historical* means "concerned with or relating to history": "Sir Walter Scott's *historical* novel *Waverly* was popular, but it wasn't *historic* in the way that Harriet Beecher Stowe's *Uncle Tom's Cabin* was."

HOBBY/PASTIME (N.)

A *hobby* is a specialized pursuit (such as coin collecting, painting, and gardening) lying outside one's regular occupation and engaged in for enjoyment or relaxation: "Solving crossword puzzles is his favorite *hobby*."

A *pastime* is any amusing activity serving to pass

time agreeably: "Listening to music with friends was his favorite *pastime*."

HOEDOWN/HOOTENANNY (N.)

A *hoedown* is a community social event featuring organized square dancing, whereas a *hootenanny* is a community social event stressing the playing of musical instruments (such as the fiddle, guitar, or piano), though dancing can also occur: "The *hootenanny* in our town was more popular than the *hoedown* because more people enjoyed playing musical instruments than square dancing."

HOG/PIG (N.)

A *hog* is an adult *pig* weighing at least 120 pounds; the term also often designates a castrated male pig raised for slaughter: "No *pig* can be a *hog* unless it's an adult."

HOME/HONE (V.)

To *home in on* is to go or return home or to be guided to a target. It is what homing pigeons and guided missiles do. To *hone* is to sharpen: "We need to *home in on* those skills we need to *hone*."

HOMICIDE/MANSLAUGHTER/MURDER (N.)

Homicide is the killing of a human being; *manslaughter* is the unlawful killing of a human being without malice; *murder* is homicide that is malicious or premeditated: "The court had to determine whether the *homicide* was *manslaughter* or *murder*."

HOMOGENIZED/PASTEURIZED (ADJ.)

In *homogenized* milk, the fat in the milk is no longer separate but part of the milk itself. *Pasteurized* milk has been subjected to a process that destroys possibly harmful bacteria: "Although *homogenized* milk has a uniform consistency, it may contain harmful bacteria not found in *pasteurized* milk."

HOMONYM/HOMOPHONE (N.)

A *homonym* is a word like another in sound and spelling but different in meaning: "*Bark* (the outside covering of a tree) and *bark* (the sound dogs make) are *homonyms*."

A *homophone* is a word pronounced the same as but different in meaning from another, regardless of whether the spelling is the same: "*Heir* and *air* are *homophones*."

HORRIBLE/HORRIFIC (ADJ.)

Horrible describes what produces either a combination of fear and loathing or pure loathing because of hideousness or hatefulness: "We could hardly imagine the *horrible* crimes committed by some of Hitler's followers."

Horrific is often used to describe what is dreadful to behold or contemplate, especially pictures, descriptions, or representations: "The movie painted a *horrific* picture of the events."

HORROR/TERROR (N.)

Horror is composed of fear, dread, and abhorrence, and is aroused by what is frightful and shocking: "The murder scene was a place of *horror*."

Terror arouses the same feelings but more intensely

and usually for a shorter amount of time: "The original *Halloween* movie was a *horror* movie, but specific scenes within it were designed to inspire *terror.*"

HORSE/MOUNT/STEED (N.)

A *horse* is a large, solid-hoofed quadrupedal herbivore, either wild or domesticated: "A palomino is a *horse* that is pale cream to gold, with a flaxen or white mane and tail."

A *mount* is a saddle *horse*—that is, a *horse* for riding: "Trigger, the *mount* ridden by Roy Rogers, died at age thirty-three."

A *steed* is a spirited *horse*, as for war: "The most famous *steed* in the American Civil War was probably Traveller, which belonged to General Robert E. Lee."

HOTEL/MOTEL (N.)

Hotels evolved from hostels, lodging places for young travelers. *Hotels* are large establishments, located mainly in cities, containing restaurants, shops, and other amenities. A *motel* is a motor *hotel*, which, unlike a *hotel*, usually provides parking next to the room and rarely has restaurants and other amenities: "People on tight budgets tend to stay at *motels* rather than *hotels*, as they usually cost less."

HUMANIST/HUMANITARIAN (N.)

A *humanist* supports humanism, a philosophy valuing human needs and rational (not religious) ways of solving human problems: "The author Isaac Asimov was a *humanist* and outspoken critic of religious supernaturalism."

A *humanitarian* is someone devoted to promoting human welfare and social reform: "Oprah Winfrey is a famous *humanitarian*."

HUMOR/WIT (N.)

Humor applies to whatever produces laughter or amusement, or the ability to perceive the ludicrous, the comical, and the absurd and to express those perceptions, usually without bitterness: "A sense of *humor* is valuable for coping with life's problems."

Wit suggests the ability to evoke laughter through remarks showing verbal dexterity or ingenuity and swift perception, especially of incongruity: "Robin Williams is famous for his *wit*."

HUN/VANDAL (N.)

The *Huns* were an Asiatic people who invaded eastern and central Europe in the fourth and fifth centuries: "Attila the *Hun* was an Asiatic invader of Europe."

Vandals were East Germanic people who ravaged Gaul, Spain, North Africa, and Rome in the fifth century: "Because the *Vandals* did much damage to the lands they ravaged in the fifth century, the word *vandal* came to designate willful or ignorant destroyers of property."

I

ILLEGAL/ILLEGITIMATE/ILLICIT (ADJ.)

What is *illegal* is contrary to or violating a law, rule, regulation, or something else—such as a custom—having the force of law: "Going the wrong way down a one-way street is *illegal*."

Illegitimate can describe offspring not recognized by law, as a child born of parents not married to each other. It can describe something illogical, such as an *illegitimate* inference or supposition, or anything contrary to law or established linguistic usage: "The author was criticized for his *illegitimate* inference."

What is *illicit* is either contrary to accepted morality (especially sexual morality) or convention, or contrary to law: "The supervisor was criticized for his *illicit* association with his secretary."

IMBUE/INFUSE/INSTILL (V.)

To *imbue* is to tinge or dye deeply (as a landscape *imbued* with shadow) or to cause to be penetrated or permeated: "The political candidate was *imbued* with patriotism."

To *infuse* is to instill into or inculcate a principle or quality: "Their parents *infused* a sense of responsibility into their children." *Infuse* can also mean "introduce," "suggest," or "insinuate": "We decided to *infuse* logic courses into several university departments."

To *instill* is either to introduce gradually or to impart: "It took years for teachers to *instill* reverence for authority into their pupils."

IMMACULATE CONCEPTION/ VIRGIN BIRTH (N.)

The *Immaculate Conception* refers to the conception of Mary, Jesus' mother, viewed as purged of Original Sin at conception. The *Virgin Birth* refers to Jesus' birth: "Although Protestants often believe in Jesus' *Virgin Birth*, they don't subscribe to Mary's *Immaculate Conception*."

IMMERSE/SUBMERGE (V.)

To *immerse* is literally to dip into liquid; figuratively, *immerse* means "engross" (*immersed* in the chess game): "I *immersed* my infected toe in hot water."

To *submerge* is to put or go under water or to cover or overflow with water; figuratively, to *submerge* is to obscure or cover up, as if under a layer of water: "The overflowing stream *submerged* part of the town."

IMMUNITY/IMPUNITY (N.)

Immunity is freedom or exemption from a duty, an obligation, or an imposition, or insusceptibility to a natural hazard (especially a disease). When it means "exemption," it's followed by *from*; when it means "insusceptibility," it's followed by *to*: "She was granted *immunity* from the tax." "He acquired *immunity* to the disease."

Impunity is exemption or freedom from punishment, harm, or loss and is often found in the expression *with impunity*: "People should not be able to commit serious crimes with *impunity*."

IMPAIR/IMPEDE (V.)

To *impair* is to weaken, damage, or worsen: "Rock 'n' roll musicians often realize that listening to loud music can *impair* hearing."

To *impede* is to interfere with, hold up, or block, suggesting slowing down or stopping motion or progress by or as if by clogging or fettering: "The numerous bureaucratic rules would *impede* our progress."

IMPENDING/PENDING (ADJ.)

Impending means imminent, with a sense of threat or menace: "We saw clouds and were concerned about the *impending* storm."

Pending is more often used to mean "not yet decided or completed": "The case was *pending* before the court."

IMPERIAL/IMPERIOUS (ADJ.)

When carrying distinct meanings, *imperial* means "pertaining to an empire or a sovereign," and *imperious* means "haughty," "domineering," or "overbearing": "We met some *imperious* aristocrats in the *imperial* palace."

IMPERSONATOR/IMPRESSIONIST (N.)

Within the context of entertainment, an *impersonator* is either a performer who imitates one particular person, such as Elvis Presley, without claiming a wide range, or a performer who pretends to be a member of the opposite sex, especially a man who pretends to be a *female*: "RuPaul gained fame in the 1990s as a female *impersonator* who sang and acted."

An *impressionist* is usually a professional performer (typically a comedian) who has developed a wide repertoire of impressions, usually of famous entertainers or politicians. The best *impressionists* have mastered not only the facial mannerisms and body language of their subjects but also their subjects' vocal qualities: "*Impressionists* will rise or fall with their ability or inability to imitate accurately the vocal qualities of their subjects."

IMPERTINENT/IMPUDENT/INSOLENT (ADJ.)

Besides meaning "irrelevant," *impertinent* implies offensively concerning oneself in another's business: "His questions were rude and *impertinent*."

Impudent means "contemptuous or cocky boldness" or "improper disregard of others": "The *impudent* young man invited himself to dinner."

Insolent implies a rude and manifest contemptuousness, suggesting a desire to insult or affront: "The man's remarks were so obscene and *insolent* that he was ejected from the auditorium."

IMPETUS/MOMENTUM (N.)

Impetus is a driving or impelling force, or an incentive or stimulus: "Getting money for each grade of A was an *impetus* for him to do better in school."

Momentum is the property of a moving body to keep moving: "The rumor began small but gained *momentum*."

IMPINGE/INFRINGE (V.)

To *impinge* is to hit, strike, or collide, whether literally or figuratively: "The bright light *impinged* on our eyes." *Impinge* can also mean "encroach" (trespass or intrude) when its meaning is close to *infringe*.

Infringe means "to intrude or trespass": "We didn't want them to *infringe* on our privacy." *Infringe* can also mean "violate" (as a law or agreement): "The U.S. government often *infringed* treaties with Native Americans."

IMPLY/INFER (V.)

The primary meaning of *imply* is "to involve as a necessary circumstance." A deed *implies* a doer, and the premises of a valid deductive argument *imply* their conclusion. By extension, *imply* can mean "to indicate or suggest something." To *infer* means "to derive by reasoning or evidence." Roughly, speakers *imply*, but hearers *infer*: "Carol did not explicitly assert her distrust of Raymond, but her words seem to *imply* it. In any event, we found it easy to *infer* the distrust."

IMPRACTICABLE/IMPRACTICAL (ADJ.)

Impracticable means "incapable of being put into practice": "His proposed solutions were so expensive as to be *impracticable*."

Impractical means either "not wise to put into or keep in practice or effect" or "incapable of dealing sensibly with practical matters": "He was learned in theoretical physics but too *impractical* to be charged with planning our trip."

INABILITY/DISABILITY (N.)

Inability is lack of power, resources, or capacity: "We didn't know about his *inability* to read."

Disability is a handicap or lack of ability because of a mental or physical defect: "Dyslexia is a common learning *disability*."

INCAPABLE/UNABLE (ADJ.)

Incapable, which means "lacking ability or qualification for some end or purpose," is followed by *of* and usually refers to a permanent or long-standing incapacity: "The bridge is *incapable* of withstanding a load of more than ten tons."

Unable means "not able," is followed by the infinitive form of a verb (for example, *to sing*), and often refers to a temporary inability: "We were *unable* to hear the speaker because we were at the rear of the auditorium."

INCENTIVE/MOTIVE (N.)

An *incentive* is something offered as a reward or prize, especially to incite or encourage action or activity: "Proportioning Christmas bonuses to workers' sales records can serve as an *incentive* for productivity."

Motives are needs, desires, and preferences that incite persons to action: "The author's desire for fame was his chief *motive* for writing."

INCHOATE/INCOHERENT (ADJ.)

Inchoate means "just begun" or "not fully formed or formulated" and often applies to thoughts or feelings: "The invention first existed only as a vague, *inchoate* idea."

Incoherent means "lacking cohesion or orderly arrangement or continuity": "Because of its contradictory elements, her explanation was *incoherent*."

INCONGRUOUS/IRONIC (ADJ.)

What is *incongruous* is inharmonious or incompatible, such as *incongruous* colors: "The two children had *incongruous* plans."

What is *ironic* will involve incongruity between how words are used and their ordinary meaning or between the actual results of a sequence of events and the normal or expected results: "When a politician who graduated from Harvard Law School refers to himself as 'a country lawyer,' his language is *ironic*."

INCUBUS/SUCCUBUS (N.)

Incubus was originally a term for an evil male spirit sexually attacking women when they slept. By extension, *incubus* has come to describe anything that oppresses or burdens like a nightmare: "Fear of being discovered weighed on the criminal's mind like an *incubus*."

Succubus was originally a term for a demon assuming female form that sexually attacked men in their sleep. The term can also designate any demon, fiend, or prostitute: "During the medieval period, many monks believed that they were attacked by *succubi*."

INCULCATE/INDOCTRINATE (V.)

To *inculcate* is to teach and impress by frequent repetition: "The boy's parents *inculcated* in him a love of literature."

To *indoctrinate* is either to give instructions (especially in fundamentals or rudiments) or to cause to be impressed with a usually partisan opinion or point of view: "The parents *indoctrinated* their children in their religion."

INEXPLICABLE/UNEXPLAINED (ADJ.)

Something *inexplicable* is incapable of explanation; something *unexplained* is something that hasn't yet been explained, though it may be capable of future explanation: "The unusual events were *unexplained* but not necessarily *inexplicable*."

INFAMOUS/NOTORIOUS (ADJ.)

Both *infamous* and *notorious* describe something well known for some disreputable or wicked quality or deed, but *infamous* emphasizes the wickedness of what is known, whereas *notorious* emphasizes the extent of the reputation: "Everyone knew that the man was a *notorious* liar who felt impelled to cover up his *infamous* deeds."

INNUENDO/INSINUATION (N.)

An *innuendo* is a veiled oblique or covert allusion (typically negative) to something not directly named. Typically, an *innuendo* relates to someone's character, ability, or some other trait. Like an *innuendo*, an *insinuation* is a covert negative hint or suggestion. The difference is that whereas *insinuation* applies chiefly to a remark or question that subtly discredits some person, *innuendo* more often applies to the method of covert suggestion rather than to particular remarks: "His *insinuations* were expressed with a cynical smile, a knowing wink, and other forms of *innuendo*."

INOCULATE/VACCINATE (V.)

To *inoculate* is to introduce microorganisms, serum, and other substances into living plants or animals. The substance introduced can be a vaccine—that is, microorganisms used in preventing or treating infectious diseases. Figuratively, to *inoculate* is to introduce something into the mind, such as ideas or attitudes: "His parents *inoculated* him with their beliefs."

To *vaccinate* is to *inoculate* with a vaccine to produce immunity to an infectious disease, such as diphtheria or typhus: "They wanted to *vaccinate* children against major childhood diseases, including measles."

INSIDIOUS/INVIDIOUS (ADJ.)

Insidious means "watching for an opportunity to entrap," "lying in wait," "intending to entrap or trick," or "having a gradual, cumulative, and often hidden effect." Accordingly, tempters, double-dealers, charlatans, plots, and even diseases can be *insidious*: "The *insidious* disease produced symptoms so gradual that it wasn't recognized until it was in its final stage."

Invidious things excite ill will, resentment, or hatred, especially when they contain or appear to contain a slight: "When a much less qualified job applicant was hired because of friendship, onlookers accused management of *invidious* hiring practices."

INSIPID/VAPID (ADJ.)

What is *insipid* is savorless (tasteless) or dull, uninteresting, or stale. In short, anything *insipid* lacks qualities that interest, stimulate, or challenge: "The mountain climber could never be satisfied with watching *insipid* TV reality shows."

What is *vapid* has lost the appeal of liveliness, freshness, or force: "The original ideas of the TV show became *vapid*."

INTELLECT/INTELLIGENCE (N.)

Intellect, sometimes interchangeable with *mind,* can designate knowing or thinking powers. Praise for people's *intellects* can specifically refer to highly competent minds good at scholarship, abstract thought, and understanding. *Intellect* often refers to powers of individual comprehension and independent thought as well as developed academic *intelligence.*

Intelligence often refers to the ability to cope with problems and challenging situations, which can characterize both human beings and nonhuman animals: "It is possible to have a great deal of *intelligence* in the sense of academic potential without having a highly developed *intellect*."

INTENSELY/INTENTLY (ADV.)

Intensely means "extremely" or "markedly": "She was *intensely* interested in language."

Intently means "earnestly," "eagerly," "engrossingly": "We listened *intently* to her anecdote."

IRIDESCENCE/LUMINESCENCE/
PHOSPHORESCENCE (N.)

Iridescence is a lustrous rainbow-like play of color, especially one caused by differential refraction of light waves, as from an oil slick, a soap bubble, fish scales, and some birds' feathers: "*Iridescence* greatly enhances the value of certain gems."

Luminescence is cool light—that is, light not due to incandescence or emissions from hot bodies. A typical household lamp uses a bulb that produces light because of a heated filament, but a fluorescent light is a product of *luminescence* because its light is not from heat but from ultraviolet rays bombarding a phosphor coating: "Fireflies produce light from *luminescence*."

Phosphorescence is *luminescence* persisting after the source is removed, as from the slow oxidation of phosphorous: "After doctors expose human tissue to ultraviolet rays, they use the resultant *phosphorescence* to diagnose some diseases."

IRONY/SATIRE (N.)

Irony, in literature, is a statement expressed in language denoting the opposite, or nearly the opposite, of what is intended, as when someone says, while a hurricane is raging, "What lovely weather!": "The man didn't intend to be taken literally, as he was using *irony*."

Satire is literary or theatrical ridicule of vice or foolishness, holding up shortcomings to censure by derision, burlesque, or *irony*, sometimes with an intent to produce improvement: "Jonathan Swift's *Gulliver's Travels* is a social and political *satire*."

J

JAIL/PRISON (N.)

Jail is the place where people awaiting trial are detained or where those convicted of minor offenses (usually those calling for detention of thirty days or under) are kept. *Prison* is a facility for housing those found guilty of major crimes to serve their terms. *Prison* is another term for *penitentiary*: "Otis, the lovable drunkard on *The Andy Griffith Show*, regularly went to *jail* but not to *prison*."

JAVELIN/LANCE (N.)

A *javelin* is a light spear thrown in war or hunting or a spearlike shaft thrown for distance in a track-and-field event: "The *javelin* throw has been part of the summer Olympics since 1908."

A *lance* is a weapon more for thrusting than for throwing, whether used by primitive people or by knights or soldiers on horseback: "A knight would have to be reasonably strong and athletic to ride horseback while using a *lance* in combat."

JOCOSE/JOCULAR/JOVIAL (ADJ.)

Jocose persons are waggish or sportive in their jesting and joking, which can often be clumsily inappropriate:

"The *jocose* man didn't realize that his jesting was inappropriate at the funeral."

Jocular persons like to amuse others by joking and are usually jolly: "The *jocular* woman derived great pleasure from entertaining others."

Jovial persons are remarkably good-humored, distinguished by their fondness for eating, drinking, and good company (conviviality): "The *jovial* man loved going to parties and dinners."

JURIST/JUROR (N.)

A *jurist* is anyone (judge, lawyer, or scholar) learned in the law: "The *jurist* was an expert in America's constitutional law."

A *juror* is a member of a jury: "A *juror* is supposed to apply the law to given factual situations and is not expected to be a *jurist*."

K

KINKY/KOOKY/QUIRKY (ADJ.)

Kinky applies to what is idiosyncratic, bizarre, and weird, with strong overtones of unconventional sexual desires or practices: "We could never have guessed that the staid-looking man had *kinky* tastes in the bedroom."

Kooky applies to people or behavior that is eccentric, offbeat, or crazy: "The historian regarded conspiracy theories as *kooky*."

Quirky designates anything eccentric, peculiar, or slightly twisted: "No one could have created the cartoon *South Park* without a *quirky* sense of humor."

KOSHER/PAREVE (ADJ.)

Kosher, in Judaism, describes what has been approved for consumption or use according to Jewish law: "The Orthodox Jew ate only *kosher* food."

Pareve (or *parve*), from Yiddish, describes food containing no milk or meat in any form and consequently meeting Jewish law for dishes that may be served with meat and dairy meals: "Because the vegetables we served weren't milk, meat, or their derivatives, they were *pareve*."

L

LADEN/LOADED (ADJ.)

To the extent that the words have similar but distinct meanings, *laden* implies being oppressed by a heavy burden, as in "a man *laden* with worry." *Loaded* (a form of the verb *load*) simply means "filled with a load": "A fully *laden* car trunk may have a back bumper close to the road, whereas a car with a *loaded* backseat is simply one that has passengers."

LAGGARD/SLUGGARD (N.)

A *laggard* is a dawdler—that is, someone who lags behind: "The rest of the group didn't want to slow down for the *laggard*."

A *sluggard* is a habitually lazy, slow-moving person: "The *sluggard* was too lazy to speed up his movements."

LAKE/POND (N.)

A *lake* is a large body of water contained within a body of land: "The largest freshwater *lake* is *Lake* Superior."

A *pond*, generally smaller than a *lake*, is also a natural body of water surrounded by land: "Because the *pond* had no place for draining off water, dying vegetation formed on its surface."

LAMB/MUTTON (N.)

A *lamb* is a young sheep, especially a sheep under one year of age. A *lamb* becomes *mutton* when the sheep is about a year old: "*Lamb* is more tender and more delicately flavored than *mutton*."

LARIAT/LASSO (N.)

Technically, a *lariat* is a rope before or after it is noosed (looped) on one end, whereas a *lasso* applies to only a rope with an adjustable loop (or noose): "The cowboy made the *lariat* into a *lasso*."

LASCIVIOUS/LECHEROUS/LEWD/ LICENTIOUS (ADJ.)

Lascivious suggests an inclination to lustfulness or a capacity for inciting lust: "The young woman was offended by the man's *lascivious* ogling."

Lecherous implies habitual indulgence of one's lust: "The *lecherous* aristocrat was driven to fulfill all his sexual fantasies."

Lewd not only implies a preoccupation with sex but also suggests grossness, vileness, and vulgarity: "The student was ejected from the class because of his *lewd* conduct."

Licentious implies a disregard for restraints on sexual conduct imposed by law or custom; the term stresses more looseness of life and habits than imperiousness of desires: "His *licentious* lifestyle made him unsuitable as headmaster of a Catholic academy."

LAWFUL/LEGAL/LEGITIMATE (ADJ.)

Lawful means "established, recognized, or sanctioned by law, including religious law, natural law, common law, civil law, and canon law." *Lawful* often means, or comes close to meaning, "allowable" or "permissible," as defined by some understood standard: "The man was the *lawful* heir."

Legal means "according to human law" and, unlike *lawful*, usually doesn't include the idea of conformity to moral principle or religious or ethical doctrine: "Sex outside marriage is *legal* in civil society."

Legitimate can mean "*legal*," "accepted by custom, tradition, or proper authorities," or "genuine": "The courts determined that the use of force by the police officers was within their *legitimate* authority."

LAY/LIE (V.)

To *lay* is to put or set in a lying position. The verb in the sense indicated takes an object: "I shall *lay* the book down if the phone rings."

To *lie* is to be in a horizontal position or to recline: "I want to *lie* down."

To make matters more confusing, the past tense of *lie* in the sense of recline is *lay*, so you'd say, "I want to *lie* down, but yesterday I *lay* down for several hours."

LECTERN/PODIUM/ROSTRUM (N.)

A *lectern* is either a reading desk with a slanted top for holding books (such as scripture) for reading (as during a church service), or a rack with a slanted top used for holding a lecturer's notes: "The professor placed his lecture notes on the *lectern*."

A *podium* is an elevated platform, as for an orchestra conductor or a public speaker: "The orchestra conductor left the *podium* after the concert was over."

A *rostrum* is an elevated platform for public speaking, but it is generally larger than a *podium* and usually bears decorations on its sides or corners: "In ancient Rome, *rostrums* were decorated with the prows of enemy ships."

LIBEL/SLANDER (N.)

Libel is the legal term for false written statements or graphic representations (such as cartoons) published or circulated without just cause or excuse, tending to expose people to public contempt, hatred, or ridicule: "The woman's malicious articles condemning John's character prompted him to accuse her of *libel*."

Slander is oral defamation: "When Paul's enemies spoke malicious lies to destroy his reputation, he sued them for *slander*."

LIGAMENT/TENDON (N.)

Ligaments are the tough connective material holding bones together. *Tendons* are the fibrous section of muscles attaching them to bones: "While the function of a *tendon* is to connect muscle to bone, the function of a *ligament* is to connect bones together."

LONELY/LONESOME (ADJ.)

A *lonely* person is one who is solitary, without company. The word can also include the idea of feeling sad because of the absence of friends or companions. It can also simply mean "isolated and rarely visited," as in a "*lonely* farmhouse in the middle of the country": "The man was alone, but he didn't always feel *lonely.*"

Lonesome is somewhat stronger and more poignant, suggesting sadness from being alone, especially after a separation or bereavement: "The first time her husband was at sea, she couldn't help feeling *lonesome.*"

LONGSHOREMAN/STEVEDORE (N.)

A *longshoreman* (related to *alongshore*) is someone employed to load and unload ships: "A *longshoreman* must be a strong, sturdy person."

A *stevedore* (derived from a Spanish word meaning "to pack" or "to stow") is an employer of *longshoremen*: "The *stevedore* hired the *longshoremen.*"

Note that in popular usage, the two terms are often used interchangeably.

LOOKING GLASS/MIRROR (N.)

A *looking glass* is a *mirror* of a particular kind— namely, one made of glass and coated on the back with quicksilver or a similar reflective amalgam: "A *looking glass* was considered more precious than a *mirror* of polished metal."

A *mirror* is a polished substance reflecting rays of light, re-creating images, though in reverse. A *mirror* is nowadays usually made of glass, but it wasn't always so: "Ancient civilizations made *mirrors* out of highly polished metals."

LUXURIANT/LUXURIOUS (ADJ.)

Anything *luxuriant* is something growing abundantly or flourishing vigorously: "We were amazed by the thickness of the *luxuriant* foliage."

Luxurious means "fond of, given to, or marked by luxury": "We were impressed by the size and accommodations of the *luxurious* hotel suite."

$\mathcal{M}$

MAGNANIMOUS/MUNIFICENT (ADJ.)

Magnanimous means "generous and noble in spirit and conduct": "A *magnanimous* person will be quick to forgive people, especially for unintentional errors."

Munificent means "generous in giving or bestowing": "We appreciated his *munificent* donation of five million dollars."

MALADROIT/MALAPROPOS (ADJ.)

Maladroit means "clumsy," whereas *malapropos* means "inappropriate": "The *maladroit* speaker made some *malapropos* statements, which offended some listeners."

MALEVOLENT/MALICIOUS/ MALIGNANT (ADJ.)

Malevolent means "having or showing intense and often vicious ill will or hatred": "We were offended by the *malevolent* gossip."

Malicious means "motivated by a desire to do evil or harm": "The harm he did was not accidental but *malicious.*"

Malignant means "evil or injurious"; "extremely *malevolent*, even to the point of rejoicing in the sufferings of others"; or, in medical usage, "severe and rapidly progressive": "John's *malignant* tumor delighted his *malignant* enemy."

MALICE/SPITE (N.)

Malice, the stronger word, is a deep-seated and often unjustified desire to hurt others. In law, it refers to a willfulness in committing crime: "The glee with which he harmed her reputation revealed *malice*."

Spite suggests petty ill will and means "envy" and "resentment": "Her belittling of her brother's awards showed *spite*."

MAUDLIN/MAWKISH (ADJ.)

Both *maudlin* and *mawkish* describe excessive sentimentality. *Maudlin* implies drunkenness, excessive emotion, or weeping: "The drunkard became *maudlin* when discussing his son's illness."

Mawkish displays of emotion are sickening, objectionable, or grossly insincere expressions of sentimentality: "Her pretending to care about the stranger was so obviously phony as to be *mawkish*."

MAY/MIGHT (AUX. V.)

To express possibility in the present tense, *may* suggests a stronger possibility than *might*: "Debbie *may* go" normally implies that she is more likely to go than "Debbie *might* go."

Because *may* also means "is allowed, or has permission," *might* is acceptable instead of *may* in some possibly ambiguous sentences: "She *may* go if she can afford it," could express either possibility or permission. The word *might* would indicate possibility.

Might is also the past tense of *may*. If you want to talk about present possibility, you'd say, "We *may* go." If you want to talk about the past, you'd say, "We thought that he *might* go." In formal usage, you'd say, "He *might* have gone had he wanted," not "He *may* have gone had he wanted."

MEMENTO/SOUVENIR (N.)

A *memento* is a keepsake of a person or an event of one's past serving to remind. A *memento* could be a locket once owned by a grandmother, a favorite watch once owned by one's father, or an autograph from a celebrity. A *souvenir* can designate a *memento*, but it is often specifically applied to products commercially created to remind people of places visited, such as picture postcards or refrigerator magnets shaped like the Empire State Building, though a *souvenir* can be a seashell from a famous beach: "Although people sometimes talk of *souvenir* shops, they normally don't talk of *memento* shops."

MEMORIAL DAY/VETERANS DAY (N.)

Memorial Day, a U.S. federal holiday observed on the last Monday of May, was originally called *Decoration Day*, founded in 1868 to pay tribute to those killed in the American Civil War. The word *decoration* referred to the practice of decorating graves with flowers. The current name of the holiday was first used in 1882, though it didn't become common until after World War II. After World War I, the focus changed from honoring those killed in the American Civil War to honoring all soldiers who had died in or as a result of any war. In 1971, *Memorial Day* became a federal holiday. Many people observe the holiday by putting flags on the graves of veterans, regardless of whether their deaths were war related: "Some Americans observe *Memorial Day* by acknowledging all loved ones who have died, veterans or not."

Veterans Day (whose name lacks an apostrophe) is observed on November 11, originally marking the first anniversary of the end of World War I (the armistice). Originally called Armistice Day, it became a federal holiday in 1938 and soon developed into a day for honoring all American veterans, living or dead.

To indicate the change of emphasis from marking the end of World War I to honoring all American soldiers, *Armistice Day* became *Veterans Day* in 1954: "Some people think that *Veterans Day* should particularly emphasize honoring living veterans to show appreciation for their commitment, distinguishing it further from *Memorial Day*."

METAPHOR/SIMILE (N.)

A *metaphor* is a figure of speech in which a word or phrase that ordinarily designates one thing is used to designate another, making an implicit comparison: "When Shakespeare wrote that all the world's a stage, he expressed what was to become a famous *metaphor*."

A *simile* is a figure of speech in which two distinctly different things are compared using the words *like* or *as*: "Saying that someone's writing is as clear as mud is a good example of a *simile*."

MILDEW/MOLD (N.)

Mildew and *molds* are fungi that form coatings on damp organic surfaces.

Mildew can form on plants, cloth, paper, and shower curtains (feeding on organic soap scum): "We soaked the shower curtain in bleach to remove *mildew*."

Mold is the fuzzy stuff forming on food that has been in the refrigerator too long. It can be green, blue, white, gray, or black, depending on exactly which type of fungus is involved. *Mold* originates from microscopic spores that settle on food when it is out in the air. The food nourishes the *mold*, which can grow and grow: "The green stuff on the stale bread is *mold*."

MODEL/PARADIGM (N.)

A *model* is a copy either on the same scale (a *model* home) or on a different scale (a *model* airplane). A *model* can also be a person serving as a pattern or source of inspiration: "His father was his *model* for self-reliance."

A *paradigm* is a model, an example, or a pattern for explaining, understanding, or demonstrating a complex process or phenomenon: "In grammar, there are *paradigms* used to explain and illustrate conjugations of verbs and declensions of nouns, pronouns, and adjectives."

MONOLOGUE/SOLILOQUY (N.)

Both *monologue* and *soliloquy* are terms for a speech made by one person alone. In *monologues*, however, speakers address others, as in the *monologues* of late-night talk show hosts, including David Letterman and Jay Leno. In *soliloquies*, speakers talk to themselves: "Shakespeare's *Hamlet* contains several *monologues* as well as Hamlet's famous *soliloquy*, containing the phrase 'to be or not to be.' "

MUSKET/RIFLE (N.)

Both are weapons, but unlike a *musket*, a *rifle* has a rifled or grooved barrel, making it a much more accurate weapon than a *musket*, which, however, was easier to reload, enabling soldiers to fire more shots in less time: "For many years, the *musket* was used in war because of its capacity for quick reloading, whereas the *rifle* was used for hunting because of its range and accuracy."

MUTINY/REVOLT (N.)

A *mutiny* is an insurrection against or willful refusal to obey existing authority, especially maritime, naval, or military authority: "A *mutiny* requires the insubordination of at least two persons resisting lawful authority."

A *revolt* can apply to a rebellion or uprising against legitimate authority: "The government needed to put down the *revolt* quickly to keep it from growing and becoming a revolution."

N

NAKED/NUDE (ADJ.)

A *naked* person is totally bare, wearing nothing; a *nude* person has become *nude* by removing clothes: "A newborn baby is *naked* at its birth, but a woman who disrobes and is a model for an artist is *nude*."

Aggression can be *naked* but never *nude*. In many other contexts, though, the terms are interchangeable.

NEOLOGISM/NONCE WORD (N.)

A *neologism* is a new word, usage, or expression. New words are created constantly, especially in science and technology: "The expression *CD-ROM*, when coined, was a *neologism*."

A *nonce word* is one coined "for the *nonce*"—that is, made up for one occasion and unlikely to be used again. Some *nonce words* can become *neologisms*, gaining regular use: "The word *quark* was originally a *nonce word* coined by James Joyce for his novel *Finnegans Wake* until physicist Murray Gell-Mann used *quark* to name a new class of subatomic particles."

The word *neologism* was itself a *neologism* in 1803, when it was coined.

NOXIOUS/OBNOXIOUS (ADJ.)

Something *noxious* is harmful or poisonous to health. The word is normally applied to physical substances, especially gas or fumes, though it's sometimes used figuratively to mean "pernicious": "We ran out of the building to avoid the *noxious* fumes."

Obnoxious things or persons are so objectionable, usually on personal grounds, that one cannot endure them with equanimity: "The man's racist speech was so *obnoxious* that we had to leave."

NUMBER/NUMERAL (N.)

A *number* is an abstract concept, whereas a *numeral* is a symbol used to express a *number*: "The Arabic *numeral* 3 and the Roman *numeral* III designate the same *number* (the concept of threeness)."

NYMPH/SYLPH (N.)

In Greek and Roman mythology, a *nymph* is a minor nature deity, represented as a beautiful maiden dwelling in mountains, forests, meadows, and waters: "A *nymph* living in woods was called a dryad."

A *sylph*, in mythology, is an imaginary or elemental being inhabiting the air. The term might have been coined by the Swiss-German physician and alchemist Paracelsus: "Just as gnomes were thought by some to inhabit subterranean Earth, so *sylphs* were thought to inhabit the air."

O

OBDURATE/OBSTINATE (ADJ.)

Obdurate is applied chiefly to people and almost always implies hardness of heart and insensitiveness to mercy, forgiveness, or help: "We asked for his forgiveness, but he was too *obdurate* to be swayed by our pleas."

Obstinate suggests persistent adherence, particularly against persuasion or challenge, to opinion, purpose, or course. The word often suggests that the persistent adherence stems more from perversity or unreasonableness than from steadfastness: "Because he wouldn't even slightly qualify his ideas in the face of serious objection, we considered him not resolute but *obstinate*."

OBSCENE/PORNOGRAPHIC (ADJ.)

What is *obscene* reflects loathsome indecency or utter obnoxiousness. It can describe coarse depictions of sexual activity, but it needn't have anything to do with sex: "Martin Luther King Jr. and his followers protested against an *obscene* system of racial segregation."

What is *pornographic* is material that is meant to stimulate sexual thoughts, produce sexual excitement, or incite sexual desire. When used negatively, the word suggests pandering to base appetite or desire: "Rather than watching a subtle, slow-moving romantic movie, the men wanted something *pornographic*."

OBSTACLE/OBSTRUCTION (N.)

An *obstacle* applies to anything standing in one's way or stopping passage: "Lack of a college education can be an *obstacle* to getting many jobs."

An *obstruction* blocks one's way or passage: "The fallen tree was an *obstruction* blocking the road."

OBTRUDE/PROTRUDE (V.)

Anything that *obtrudes* is thrust forward, presented, or called to notice without warrant or request. It can mean "to thrust out," as when a snail *obtrudes* a tentacle. When people *obtrude*, they are unduly imposing themselves on something else: "I shall not *obtrude* my nose where it doesn't belong."

Anything that *protrudes* sticks out, especially in an unusual or unexpected way: "We saw envelopes *protruding* from his shirt pocket."

OBVERSE/REVERSE (N.)

Even though the word *obverse* seems as if it should designate something secondary, it refers, in numismatics, to the main side of a coin, typically "the heads." The opposite side is the *reverse*, or "the tails." Although most coins have heads on the *obverse*, or main side, not all do. Some older coins have sides that look so much alike that it is difficult to determine the main side: "On the Lincoln penny, Lincoln's image is on the *obverse*, and the Lincoln Memorial is on the *reverse*."

OBVIATE/PREVENT (V.)

To *obviate* is to make unnecessary, often suggesting prudently or intelligently removing obstacles or difficulties: "I deliberately made enough money to *obviate* financial worries."

To *prevent* is to create an insurmountable obstacle or impediment to some event or condition: "Always checking whether you're holding your keys before shutting your car door will *prevent* your being locked out of your car."

OCCUPIED/PREOCCUPIED (ADJ.)

If you're *occupied*, you're busy or employed: "I was unable to help because I was *occupied* at work."

If you're *preoccupied*, you're engrossed or lost in thought: "The worker was too *preoccupied* with the needs of her children to notice that the man needed help."

OCEAN/SEA (N.)

The *ocean* is a saltwater body covering almost three quarters of Earth's surface. That body is divided into such areas as the Atlantic *Ocean*, Pacific *Ocean*, Indian *Ocean*, Arctic *Ocean*, and Antarctic (or Southern) *Ocean*: "The Pacific *Ocean* is the world's largest body of water."

Although *sea* is sometimes loosely applied to the *ocean*, *sea* more precisely represents a saltwater body that is part of an *ocean* or that opens into an *ocean*, including the Black *Sea*, Mediterranean *Sea*, Red *Sea*, and Sargasso *Sea*: "The Mediterranean, a *sea* of the Atlantic *Ocean*, is almost completely enclosed by land."

ODIOUS/OPPROBRIOUS (ADJ.)

Anything or anyone *odious* arouses or deserves hatred or repugnance: "The man was hated for his *odious* crime."

Any *opprobrious* conduct brings or deserves disgrace, and any *opprobrious* language expresses offensive reproach or scorn: "He was condemned for his receiving of a bribe and other *opprobrious* conduct."

OPHTHALMOLOGIST/OPTICIAN/ OPTOMETRIST (N.)

An *ophthalmologist* is a medical doctor (MD) who may perform eye exams and eye surgery. *Ophthalmologists*, who must understand the relationship between the eyes and the rest of the body, complete at least twelve years of school, including college, medical school, and residency: "The *ophthalmologist* regularly tests Debbie's eye pressure for symptoms of glaucoma."

An *optician* is a professional who has normally received at least two years of technical training to fulfill prescriptions for corrective eyewear. *Opticians* are trained to prepare and adjust glasses; additional training is needed to dispense contact lenses: "The *optician* fitted me for glasses."

Optometrists are doctors of optometry (OD) but aren't doctors of medicine (MD). Each typically has an undergraduate degree of science followed by a four-year optometry degree. They are trained to conduct eye exams, fit patients for contact lenses, and diagnose infections and disorders. They are trained in eye anatomy and physiology, and can handle preoperative and postoperative care and prescribe treatments: "The *optometrist* tested my vision to see whether I needed a new prescription for my glasses."

OSCILLATE/UNDULATE (V.)

To *oscillate* is to swing back and forth like a pendulum, literally or figuratively: "I like electric fans that *oscillate*, blowing air within a wide range."

To *undulate* is to move in a wavelike motion, or to rise and fall in volume, pitch, or cadence: "Many women attract attention when they *undulate* their hips."

OUTLAW/SCOFFLAW (N.)

An *outlaw* is a lawless person or a fugitive from the law: "Jesse James was an *outlaw*, whose crimes have inspired many books."

A *scofflaw* is a contemptuous lawbreaker—especially of minor laws, such as parking regulations: "The *scofflaw* had four parking tickets and ignored them all."

P

PART/PORTION/PROPORTION (N.)

A *part* is something less than a whole, or a constituent of a whole: "We liked visiting that *part* of town."

A *portion* is a *part* given for a purpose or a share of something: "My *portion* of the inheritance was less than yours."

A *proportion* is a *part* in relation to a whole: "We were surprised by the *proportion* of women in the class."

PARTAKE/PARTICIPATION (V.)

Although both words mean "to take a part or share," *partake* is primarily used to describe taking a share of something (especially food or drink), and *participate* describes joining in an activity with other people: "Both *partook* of fresh bread before they *participated* in the ceremony."

PARTIALLY/PARTLY (ADV.)

Partially means "in part or parts" or "in some measure or degree": "His efforts were *partially* successful."

Partly means "not completely": "He may not be completely at fault, but he is *partly* to blame for the accident."

The distinction is subtle, but the idea is that *partly* is used to refer to a part in relation to an identifiable whole, whereas *partially* emphasizes the extent of a quality.

PEACEABLE/PEACEFUL (ADJ.)

Peaceable describes persons who are peace loving— that is, disposed to avoid strife and to keep peace: "The people in the village were *peaceable* and would almost never argue."

Peaceful applies especially to a life, condition or state, period or age, or nation in which peace prevails, but can apply to whatever indicates peace, especially of mind: "It is easier to have a *peaceful* mind if one is living in a *peaceful* environment."

PEOPLE/PERSONS (N.)

People is a term collectively referring to human beings as against, say, dogs or lions: "Only *people* can become president."

Persons signifies humans in their individualizing external aspects, including their bodies, features, and clothing. Further, one should use the word *persons* when specifying precise numbers: "There are seven *persons* in our party."

PERMEATE/PERVADE (ADJ.)

When used most literally, *permeate* implies spreading completely through a substance or flowing through or penetrating every pore or space: "The dye *permeated* the fabric."

Pervade suggests diffusion through every part of

a whole and is often applied to places, writings, and works of art rather than to purely physical things: "The importance of the individual *pervades* the Bill of Rights in the U.S. Constitution."

PERTINACIOUS/TENACIOUS (ADJ.)

Pertinacious suggests determined resolution in purpose, belief, or action, but often includes the suggestion of irksomeness; a *pertinacious* person often irritates others: "We were annoyed by the *pertinacious* beggar."

Tenacious implies determined adherence to a position or course of action despite all opposing forces and is often used positively: "We applauded her *tenacious* devotion to earning her doctorate."

Tenacious, unlike *pertinacious*, can describe strength of retentiveness, as in "a *tenacious* memory."

PERVERSE/PERVERTED (ADJ.)

A *perverse* person willfully refuses either to do what is right, customary, or lawful or to believe what is true or correct: "In his *perverse* mood, he was resistant to any guidance."

A *perverted* person is regarded as having twisted or distorted something in such a way as to produce corruption: "The child molester engaged in *perverted* acts."

PHANTASM/PHANTASMAGORIA/ PHANTOM (N.)

A *phantasm* is something that is apparently seen but that has no physical reality, including ghosts and illusory mental images: "The scientist told us that whatever we imagined we saw was a mere *phantasm*."

A *phantasmagoria* is a fantastic sequence of haphazardly associated imagery (as in dreams or feverish hallucinations) or a constantly changing medley of real or imagined images: "The *phantasmagoria* of the music video was suggestive of an LSD trip."

A *phantom* can be a ghost or anything seeming to exist physically but existing only as an illusion or as a product of imagination: "Dream images, mirages, and optical illusions are all *phantoms*."

PILLORY/STOCKS (N.)

Both *pillory* and *stocks* refer to similar forms of humiliating public punishment. A *pillory* consists of a wooden frame with holes in which the head and hands are locked. The *stocks* consist of a wooden frame with holes in which the feet or feet and hands are locked: "A *pillory* was more severe and dangerous than the *stocks* because a *pillory* could suffocate short persons, who would be suspended by their necks."

PITIABLE/PITIFUL (ADJ.)

What is *pitiable* either deserves or excites pity or evokes pity mingled with contempt (especially because of inadequacy): "The teacher was angered by the student's *pitiable* excuse for not completing his homework."

Pitiful describes what excites pity or, sometimes, commiseration because it is felt to be deeply pathetic: "We were saddened by her *pitiful* financial situation."

PLAN/SCHEME (V.)

To *plan* suggests engaging in a course of action well thought through and possibly even expressed in writing: "We sat down to *plan* our vacation."

To *scheme* often suggests secret methods motivated by craftiness or methods used for underhanded aims: "The criminals decided to *scheme* against the gang leader."

PLAQUE/TARTAR (N.)

If your teeth are covered with gelatinous film containing saliva and bacteria, it's *plaque*: "We brush regularly to minimize *plaque*."

If the *plaque* accumulates, it forms *tartar* (or dental calculus), a harder, brownish yellow deposit of food particles and salts, such as phosphate and calcium carbonate: "The dental hygienist scaled my teeth to remove *tartar*."

POSTAL CARD/POSTCARD (N.)

You buy a *postal card*, a 3- by $5\frac{1}{8}$-inch card with postage printed on the front and the message side blank, at a U.S. post office: "The price of a *postal card* increased when the price of first-class stamps increased."

You can buy a *postcard* or a picture *postcard*, of varying sizes, at many commercial establishments, especially those connected with tourism: "We bought *postcards* at the university's bookstore."

PRACTICABLE/PRACTICAL (ADJ.)

Practicable means "capable of being put into practice": "Her plans were so expensive that they weren't *practicable*."

Practical means "concerned with actual practice," "useful in practice," or "guided by practical experience and observation rather than theory": "She was a *practical* woman seeking *practical* solutions."

PRECIPITATE/PRECIPITOUS (ADJ.)

Although the two adjectives stem from the same root, *precipitate* means "hasty" or "rash," whereas *precipitous* refers to physical steepness or a sharp decline and means "of or like a precipice" or "dangerously steep." Mountain cliffs and declines in the stock market can be *precipitous*: "The decision to camp out near the *precipitous* cliff was *precipitate*."

PREEMPT/PREVENT (V.)

To *preempt* is to do or say something before others, to make their words or actions unnecessary or ineffective: "The politician who was accused of employing a prostitute held a press conference to *preempt* criticism from journalists."

To *prevent* is to stop some action or event from happening without the idea of doing something first: "I returned my library book on time to *prevent* late charges."

PRELIMINARY/PREPARATORY (ADJ.)

What is *preliminary* serves as a preceding event or introduces what follows: "The *preliminary* speaker introduced the main speaker."

What is *preparatory* prepares for what follows: "Normally, having a high school diploma or its equivalent is *preparatory* for college entrance."

PREMONITION/PRESENTIMENT (N.)

A *premonition* is a strong feeling, without a rational basis, that something (usually undesirable) is going to happen, or an early warning. A *premonition* often suggests that those receiving it can possibly take steps to prevent its fulfillment: "Because she had a *premonition* that her plane would crash, she took the train."

A *presentiment* is a feeling that something (often bad) is about to occur. The feeling of a *presentiment* (as opposed to a *premonition*) isn't necessarily a warning, nor is there any suggestion that the person having the *presentiment* can prevent or avoid its fulfillment: "The lawyer had a *presentiment* that the judge would rule against his client."

PREROGATIVE/PRIVILEGE (N.)

A *prerogative* is an exclusive or special right or power, especially one belonging to an office, a position, or an official body: "One *prerogative* of an American president is to grant pardons to people convicted of federal crimes."

A *privilege* is a special benefit or advantage that someone enjoys: "Well-behaved prisoners are sometimes given *privileges* other prisoners don't have."

PRESUMPTIVE/PRESUMPTUOUS (ADJ.)

Presumptive beliefs are those having reasonable grounds, even though they may be false: "She is the *presumptive* nominee."

Presumptuous means "overstepping due bounds, as of propriety or courtesy, as in taking liberties": "It was *presumptuous* of me to invite myself to dinner."

PRETENSE/PRETENSION/
PRETENTIOUSNESS (N.)

A *pretense* is a claim made or implied, especially when it isn't supported by fact; a false show; or a professed rather than real intention or purpose: "His claiming to love his wife was mere *pretense*."

A *pretension*, like a *pretense*, is an allegation of doubtful value, as in a pretext, but it is also an aspiration or intention that may or may not be realized: "She has serious literary *pretensions*."

Pretentiousness usually suggests an ostentatious display or an appearance of importance unjustified by a thing's value or a person's standing: "Given the *pretentiousness* with which the man spoke, one would think that he was the leader of some country rather than an ordinary person."

PRETENSE/PRETEXT (N.)

A *pretense* is a false show of something, as when people pretend to be much more influential than they are; it needn't involve literal lies, though it could, as when people gain advantages under false *pretenses*: "His appearing to be rich was mere *pretense*."

A *pretense* can be professed by a false reason or motive, in which case it is a *pretext*, which involves offering false reasons or motives to excuse or explain behavior: "The men would use any *pretext* to avoid work."

PRIDEFUL/PROUD (ADJ.)

A *prideful* person is excessively haughty: "The minister said that people need to respect themselves but shouldn't be *prideful*."

Proud people are pleased with themselves and their achievements: "Aristotle believed that noble people are properly *proud* of themselves."

PRIM/PRISSY (ADJ.)

A *prim* person is affectedly precise or proper, stiffly formal, and so fastidious in manners and morals as to displease observers: "His grandmother is so *prim* and proper that we find it impossible to relax around her, lest we should offend her sensibilities."

Prissy, though close to *prim* in meaning, means "fussily *prim*" and connotes sissiness, suggesting an exaggerated sense of what is proper or precise: "On the 1960s TV show *Lost in Space*, the character of Dr. Smith came to develop a *prissy* exterior while remaining dishonest and treacherous."

PRIMEVAL/PRIMORDIAL (ADJ.)

There are contexts in which *primeval* and *primordial* are interchangeable, but they can sometimes be distinguished.

In its basic sense, *primeval* applies to something belonging to or characteristic of the first ages of the Earth. The word, however, often simply suggests extreme antiquity or the absence of all signs of human trespass or influence: "They were city people who had no experience of *primeval* forests."

Primordial describes the starting point in a course of growth or development, or the earliest stage in order or formation: "Life eventually came out of the *primordial* ooze."

PROCLIVITY/PROPENSITY (N.)

Both words signify a natural tendency or inclination, but *proclivity* often implies a tendency toward evil (as defined by the speaker or writer). Even when *proclivity* is used without negative implications, it still implies stronger and less controllable urges than those associated with *propensity*: "The evangelist insisted that human beings are born with a *proclivity* toward evil."

People have a *propensity* toward or for something when they have an innate or inherent desire for it or feel driven to experience or do it: "Like most young children, he had a *propensity* for immediate gratification."

PROCURE/SECURE (V.)

Procure and *secure* can be interchangeable when they mean "to come into possession of," though there are contexts and idioms that require one or the other.

Procure is likely to suggest acquiring through planning and contriving over time, sometimes using unspecified or even questionable means. Accordingly, *procure* sometimes means "obtain for prostitution," and pimps are sometimes called, or call themselves, *procurers*: "We have no idea how the criminals *procured* their weapons."

Secure may suggest acquiring for safe lasting possession, as when one *secures* tickets for the Super Bowl. It may also suggest gaining what is hard to come by because of rarity or competition: "Because of the current housing market, they found it difficult to *secure* a loan."

PURPOSEFULLY/PURPOSELY (ADV.)

When you do something *purposefully*, you do it with determination and with its purpose clearly in mind: "He climbed the mountain *purposefully*."

When you do something *purposely*, you do it by design or on purpose: "His brothers claimed that he *purposely* knocked over the vase."

Q

QUAKE/QUAVER/QUIVER (V.)

To *quake* is to shake or tremble: "They became frightened when the building *quaked*."

Quaver sometimes suggests irregular vibration or fluctuation, especially as an effect of something that disturbs, as when a breeze causes the flames of streetlamps to *quaver*. *Quaver*, though, often implies tremulousness, or a fearful trembling, especially when it is applied to voices or utterances affected by weakness or emotion: "The elderly woman's voice began to *quaver*."

Quiver often applies to visible vibration and suggests a slight, rapid shaking, comparable to the vibration of the strings of musical instruments: "We heard the leaves *quiver* in the wind."

QUIESCENT/QUIET (ADJ.)

Quiescent can mean "marked by inactivity or tranquil repose," "causing no symptoms" (a *quiescent* tumor), or "being quiet or still": "A disease may be *quiescent* and later manifest symptoms."

Quiet may imply absence of perceptible motion,

sound, or both, but it tends to suggest also the absence of excitement or turbulence and the presence of serenity or tranquillity: "The emphasis on the absence of sound distinguishes *quiet* from *quiescent*."

R

RAIN/SHOWERS (N.)

If the forecast is for *rain*, forecasters expect the *rain* to fall steadily and from a flat, stratus type of cloud, not changing much in intensity from hour to hour. If the forecast is for *showers*, the rain will be intermittent, be somewhat scattered, vary in intensity over just a short time, fall from a cumulus type of cloud, and usually cover less area than what would be covered by *rain*: "The steady flow of light *rain* is for many people better sleeping weather than intermittent *showers*."

RANT/RAVE (V.)

To *rant* is to talk or scold violently: "The teacher began to *rant* at her students for not doing their homework."

To *rave* can mean "to talk wildly in or as if in delirium" or "to talk with extreme, rapturous enthusiasm." *Rave* can, then, sometimes suggest irrationality or madness: "The robber flew into a rage and began to *rave* when one of his victims called him a worthless parasite."

RARE/SCARCE (ADJ.)

Both *rare* and *scarce* are applied to what is found only occasionally or in small amounts, and may sometimes be interchangeable: "That level of conscientious service from a merchant is *rare* [or *scarce*]."

Although *rare* can describe what is uncommon, it can also emphasize the idea that something is both unusual and valuable: "The museum was allowed to display the *rare* painting for only three weeks."

Scarce can simply mean "insufficient to meet a demand or existing in short supply": "Blueberries are *scarce* this year."

RASCAL/ROGUE/SCOUNDREL (N.)

Currently, a *rascal* can be applied playfully to a pleasingly mischievous person: "Your five-year-old boy is quite a *rascal*." The word *rascal* has described, and can still describe, a person of base dishonesty: "Some *rascal* defrauded the widow of her inheritance."

Rogue often suggests the wiliness of a vagabond, though it can be applied to someone playfully mischievous. A *rogue's* gallery, by the way, is a collection of pictures of known and suspected criminals maintained by police: "The *rogue* moved from town to town, swindling honest citizens."

A *scoundrel* is often used to describe a worthless, mean, and unscrupulous person: "In the movie *The Departed*, Jack Nicholson portrayed a *scoundrel* who would stop at nothing to get what he wanted."

In order of villainy, a *scoundrel* describes the most wicked and *rascal* (in some contexts) the least wicked.

RAVAGE/RAVISH (V.)

To *ravage* is to destroy or devastate and often refers to the violent, severe, and often cumulative destruction produced by depredations, raids, fires, storms, or flood: "The fire *ravaged* the forest."

Ravish has diverse meanings. It can mean "to rape," "to seize and carry away by force," or "to enchant or enrapture." (It is sometimes misused to mean "extremely hungry" or "famished.") An example of its positive meaning: "His eyes were *ravished* by the beauty of the rose garden."

REBUFF/REBUT/REFUTE (V.)

To *rebuff* is to snub or reject (especially sympathy or offers of help), or to beat back or reject an attack: "He *rebuffed* our offer of help."

To *rebut* is to try to disprove some proposition and is often used within the context of debates or courts of law. *Rebut* implies the offering of reasons or evidence to try to disprove a proposition but doesn't imply that the attempt at disproof is successful: "The politician tried to *rebut* the accusations."

Refute includes the idea of successful disproof or falsification: "The man *rebutted* the accusation by citing evidence against it, but his evidence fell short of disproving the accusation and so didn't *refute* it."

REBUKE/REPRIMAND/REPROACH/ REPROVE (V.)

Rebuke implies a sharp and severe expression of disapproval: "The judge *rebuked* the criminal for his habitual offenses."

Reprimand suggests a reproof that is formal and often public or official: "The teacher *reprimanded* the child for talking during her lecture."

Reproach implies a mild scolding, often emphasizing the displeasure of the scolder: "His mother *reproached* him for leaving his library books at home."

Reprove suggests a kindly intent to correct a fault: "His mother told us that she wouldn't spank her son, but she would *reprove* him for his rude remarks."

Note that although people may be said to *reproach* themselves, feeling regret about their conduct, or may be *reproved* by their consciences, they can only normally be *rebuked* and perhaps also *reprimanded* by others.

RECANT/RETRACT (V.)

To *recant* is to withdraw or repudiate one's former belief or statement, especially a religious or political one, publicly or formally, in an admission of error: "The man became a Protestant and *recanted* his former belief in the authority of the Roman Catholic Church."

Retract is an action that is less formal than that which *recant* describes. *Retract* means "to take back" (as a confession), "to refuse to abide by" (as an agreement), "to go back on" (as a promise), or "to draw back" (as when a cat *retracts* its claws): "We found it incredible that the man *retracted* his confession."

RECOUP/RECOVER (V.)

To *recoup* is to retrieve, usually in equivalent rather than identical form, something lost (especially money): "She *recouped* her losses in the stock market."

To *recover* is to get back anything (material or nonmaterial) that was lost: "When he *recovered* the Rolex watch his wife gave him, he *recovered* his peace of mind."

REDUNDANT/REPETITIOUS (ADJ.)

When repetition becomes superfluous, it is *redundant*. Although *redundant* can apply to anything superfluous, in its specific application to words, the term describes a superfluity resulting from repetitiousness and the use of unnecessary words: "In nonlegal writing, the expression *cease and desist* is *redundant*."

When repetition becomes boring, it is *repetitious*: "The boy was bored by his teacher's *repetitious* instructions."

REFLECTION/REFRACTION (N.)

Regarding light, *reflection* is the throwing back of a ray, whereas *refraction* is the bending of a ray: "You can see your *reflection* in a mirror because of the *reflection* of light waves." "The *refraction* of light waves explains why a stick partially immersed in water looks bent."

REFURBISH/REMODEL (V.)

To *refurbish* is to brighten or freshen up: "He *refurbished* the old table by sandpapering and waxing it."

To *remodel* is to make over again or rebuild: "The house was *remodeled* in the original style."

REGAL/ROYAL (ADJ.)

Anything *regal* is splendid, magnificent, or befitting royalty. It can literally refer to a king or his office but is especially used to refer to splendidness associated with royalty: "We knew he was wealthy, but we were impressed by his *regal* estate."

Royal describes anything associated with kings,

queens, or the crown, without necessarily implying magnificence: "Prince William receives a great deal of attention because he is a member of the English *royal* family."

REGRET/REMORSE (N.)

To experience *regret* is to feel sorry about something previously done or said that now appears wrong, mistaken, or hurtful to others. To experience *regret* can also refer to a sadness, disappointment, or longing for something or someone no longer there: "A person can feel *regret* for the loss of a relationship without believing that anyone was at fault for the loss."

To feel *remorse* is to feel guilt, a gnawing distress due to a sense of guilt for past wrongs. *Remorse* involves self-reproach that can be absent from *regret*, which can sometimes involve a sadness that things didn't turn out better. *Remorse* suggests a prolonged and insistent self-reproach and anguish for past wrongs, especially for those with irremediable consequences: "Some criminals can commit horrible crimes with no obvious *remorse*."

REPELLENT/REPUGNANT/REPULSIVE (ADJ.)

Something *repellent* is so disgusting that it drives people away: "She would avoid violent movies because she found them *repellent*."

Something *repugnant* is so contrary and offensive to one's ideas, principles, or tastes that it stirs up resistance and loathing: "To Dr. Martin Luther King Jr., as to millions of other Americans, racial segregation was *repugnant*."

Something *repulsive* tends to produce a strong physical aversion: "General Eisenhower, seeing evidence of Nazi atrocities, found the experience so *repulsive* he threw up."

REPRESS/SUPPRESS (V.)

To *repress* is to check or restrain, either by an external force, or by the power of the will or mind. It often suggests that the thing held back may break out again. When referring to self-imposed restraint, especially against powerful urges, *repress*, not *suppress*, is the word: "The man found it difficult to *repress* his unconventional sexual urges."

To *suppress* strongly implies putting down or keeping back completely, usually with great or oppressive force or even violence: "The dictator *suppressed* any public criticism of his policies."

REQUIREMENT/REQUISITE (N.)

A *requirement* can imply something wanted, needed, or demanded, often as a condition. The term is often used to describe what is arbitrarily demanded or expected, especially by those laying down conditions, as for admission to college, enlistment in military service, or membership in an organization: "Taking the SAT was a *requirement* for admission to the university."

Requisite is the customary term for something indispensable to the end in view or necessitated by a thing's nature and not arbitrarily demanded: "The freedom to question the government publicly is a *requisite* for any free society."

RESIN/ROSIN (N.)

Resin is a substance that is usually gummy when warm but hard and brittle when cold. Transparent or translucent, this yellowish to brownish substance can occur naturally from plant life (such as pine trees) or can be manufactured. *Resins* are used in shellacs and varnishes, in pipe mouthpieces, in electrical insulators, and even in medicines: "We got the *resin* from the pine tree."

Rosin is a hard, brittle *resin* used on the bows of string instruments, the hands of gymnasts, and the shoes of ballerinas to prevent slipping: "The gymnast applied *rosin* to his hands before approaching the parallel bars."

RESTIVE/RESTLESS (ADJ.)

Restive means "uneasily impatient under restriction, opposition, criticism or delay," "resisting control," or "refusing to move." People can be *restive* in their resistance to control, but the term is often used to describe animals, especially horses: "The *restive* horse wasn't about to budge."

Restless means "impatient," "nervous," or "unable to rest or relax": "The man was too *restless* to fall asleep."

RETORT/RIPOSTE (N.)

A *retort* is a quick, incisive reply to a criticism or putdown, especially when the reply turns the critic's remarks to the advantage of the one giving the *retort*: "The stand-up comic offered a powerful *retort* to the heckler."

A *riposte* is a quick, incisive reply but it is less strong than a *retort* and doesn't emphasize the anger or wit associated with *retort*. What's more, a *riposte* can designate any retaliatory action or maneuver, including a quick thrust in fencing after parrying an opponent's lunge: "His *riposte* was clever but was less effective than the original put-down."

REVENGE/VENGEANCE (N.)

Revenge implies vindictive retaliation: "Each side wanted *revenge* for previous acts of violence."

Vengeance implies just retribution: "The Bible states that to God alone belongs *vengeance*."

REVEREND/REVERENT/
REVERENTIAL (ADJ.)

Reverend means "deserving reverence," as when people are entitled to respect or honor because of their age or position: "The position of a federal judge is a *reverend* position." *Reverend* is often found in the title of members of clergy, where convention demands that it be followed by a title (Mr. or Dr.), a first name or an initial, and a last name: "The *Reverend* Mr. Thomas Smith visited the hospital to comfort the sick."

Reverent means "showing or feeling reverence," where the reverence is sincere: "We were impressed by the young man's *reverent* manners."

Reverential means "showing (but not necessarily feeling) reverence": "Her manners around the celebrity were more than polite; they were *reverential*."

REVOLVE/ROTATE (V.)

To *revolve* is to travel in a circle or around a central point: "The Earth *revolves* around the Sun."

To *rotate* is to spin or turn on an axis: "The Earth *rotates* on its polar axis."

RIFLE/RIFFLE (V.)

To *rifle* is to search through, especially to steal and carry off, and usually takes as its object a place, building, treasury, or receptacle: "The burglars *rifled* the strongbox."

To *riffle* is to flick or leaf through (as papers or the pages of a book). It can describe also shuffling playing cards, especially by separating them into two halves and mixing them using one's thumbs: "I *riffled* through the book, looking for the relevant page."

RIGOROUS/VIGOROUS (ADJ.)

Rigorous applies to people, their actions, their way of life, or the conditions under which people or animals live. It means "characterized by severity or harshness" or "rigidly demanding or accurate": "The penguins in the South Pole live in a *rigorous* climate."

Vigorous suggests active strength, force, vitality, and robustness of body or strength of mind: "The *vigorous* man had no problem following the exercise regimen."

RITE/RITUAL (N.)

A *rite* describes the prescribed action of a special formal occasion, especially an important or unusual one: "The fraternity of masons teach their members specific *rites*."

Ritual, in its older sense, describes the entire *rites* of service or faith, as in "The Roman Catholic *ritual* impressed them." More often today *ritual* designates any series of actions given unusual importance and a prescribed order: "We understand the funeral *ritual* and the importance it attaches to the form and order of events."

RUCKUS/RUCTION/RUMPUS (N.)

A *ruckus* is a disturbance or commotion: "We went downstairs to see what the *ruckus* was about."

A *ruction* is a riotous disturbance or a noisy quarrel: "The *ruction* between John and Susan stemmed from John's refusal to dress up for the dinner guests."

A *rumpus* is a noisy clamor, suggesting even greater disturbance than a row (noisy quarrel) because it connotes uproar: "The *rumpus* was so loud that everyone in the restaurant heard it."

RURAL/RUSTIC (ADJ.)

Rural, in its widest meaning, describes open country, whether uninhabited or sparsely populated. It suggests agricultural pursuits or simple community life. *Rural* suggests the pleasant aspects of country life, whereas *rustic* often carries with it the suggestion of lacking polish, sophistication, and refinement: "We liked the fresh air and quiet of our *rural* environment, but felt uncomfortable around *rustic* manners."

S

SALARY/WAGES (N.)

A *salary* is a form of fixed compensation regularly paid (as by the year, quarter, month, or week) for services and usually expressed in monthly or annual terms: "My *salary* increased from fifty thousand to a hundred thousand dollars a year."

Wages are earnings based on hourly, daily, weekly, or piecework performance: "My temporary job pays *wages* of fifteen dollars per hour."

SALUBRIOUS/SALUTARY (ADJ.)

What is *salubrious* promotes health: "We got fewer colds when we moved to a *salubrious* climate."

What is *salutary* promotes an improvement, especially an educational, a psychological, or a moral one: "Associating with positive people had a *salutary* effect on my mood."

SARCASTIC/SARDONIC (ADJ.)

Sarcastic language derides, contemptuously taunts, or expresses ridicule intending to hurt others' feelings: "The speaker's *sarcastic* jibes at gun owners alienated some members of the audience."

Sardonic comments or expressions carry scorn or bitterness along with skepticism or cynicism: "The TV interviewer's *sardonic* question to the wealthy televangelist was whether Jesus also needed one-thousand-dollar suits."

SATED/SATIATED/SATURATED (ADJ.)

Although both *sated* and *satiated* can refer merely to being completely satisfied in one's appetites, they often refer to an unpleasant overfilling or overfeeding. The idea of satisfaction to the point of excess is associated even more with *satiated* than with *sated*: "The water *sated* [satisfied] my thirst, but the two-pound steak *satiated* me, giving me a feeling of being stuffed."

Saturated can mean "thoroughly soaked" or "filled to capacity": "The market for fast-food restaurants in my town is *saturated*."

SCANT/SCANTY/SCARCE/SPARSE (ADJ.)

Scant means "barely sufficient" and suggests a falling short of what is desirable rather than of what is necessary or essential. The word is usually applied to abstract nouns: "He made the decision with *scant* regard for its long-term consequences."

Scanty suggests a falling short of what is essential rather than what is desirable: "If they don't supplement their *scanty* income, they won't have enough money to pay their bills."

Scarce describes something valuable in short supply or infrequently seen or found: "Gasoline was *scarce* in our city after the hurricane."

Sparse describes what is not dense or crowded: "There are many areas of Wyoming with *sparse* populations."

SCOFF/SNEER (V.)

Scoff implies a derision based on insolence, irreverence, lack of respect, or incredulity: "Their disbelief led them to *scoff* at talk of a miraculous remedy."

More than *scoff*, *sneer* implies a strong cynicism and ill-natured contempt. When someone says something while *sneering*, the suggestion is that he or she is saying something caustic with a scornful or derisive facial expression or tone of voice: "His scornful expression perfectly complemented his caustic remark as he *sneered* at my suggestions."

SCORN/SHUN/SPURN (V.)

To *scorn* is to show indignant or profound contempt: "Thomas Paine *scorned* the concentration of political power in the hands of a few."

To *shun* is to avoid a person or thing deliberately and usually habitually: "The lazy man *shunned* work."

To *spurn* is to reject with contempt: "She *spurned* all offers of reconciliation."

SCREENPLAY BY/STORY BY/ WRITTEN BY (ATTR.)

A *screenplay by* credit will go to those who wrote the scenes and dialogue of a screenplay but normally didn't generate the idea for the story: "Those receiving *screenplay by* credit need to be good at writing dialogue but not necessarily good at coming up with broad organizing themes and basic plots."

A *story by* credit will go to those who came up with the essence of a movie (such as its plot or main characters) and who might have written a treatment or summary, but who didn't write the screenplay. Similarly, those receiving a screen *story by* credit have adopted material from others' novels, short stories, or news articles for film, often making substantial changes: "The author of the novel was infuriated by the changes made by those receiving screen *story by* credits for the movie based on her book."

A *written by* credit will go to those who both conceived the story and wrote the screenplay, usually merging the meaning of *story by* and *screenplay by*: "There are some writers like Woody Allen, who are so creative and talented that they can conceive original ideas and write screenplays based on them, resulting in a *written by* credit."

SCRIMP/SKIMP (V.)

Scrimp, used chiefly of money and material goods, means "to be frugal," "to economize severely," or "to be excessively sparing with or of": "The millionaire we met once felt the need to *scrimp* and save."

Skimp is normally used to mean "give insufficient attention to," though it can mean "to be stingy or very thrifty": "In studying for a test, it is a mistake simply to reread lecture notes while *skimping* rehearsal of the material."

SCYTHE/SICKLE (N.)

The *scythe* and the *sickle* are tools for cutting grass, crops, or weeds. Whereas a *scythe* has a long handle and can be used while standing erect, a *sickle* has a short handle, requiring the user to bend over to cut with it: "Because of her lower back pain, she preferred using the *scythe* to using the *sickle*, obviating the need for bending her body."

SEASONABLE/SEASONAL (ADJ.)

Seasonable describes whatever is suitable for a season: "We enjoyed the *seasonable* temperatures of fall."

Seasonal describes whatever is caused by a season: "We experience *seasonal* unemployment during the winter at our local oceanfront."

SEDATE/STAID (ADJ.)

Sedate describes composure and decorous seriousness in character or speech, often suggesting the avoidance of lightness or frivolity: "The headmaster of the New England academy had the bearing of a *sedate* aristocrat."

Staid is stronger than *sedate* and implies a settled sedateness, a prim self-restraint, and an even stronger rejection of lightness or frivolity: "The mathematician-philosopher Bertrand Russell grew up in a *staid* Victorian home, where discipline and duty were dominant."

SEDITION/TREASON (N.)

Sedition is action against a government to which one owes allegiance. It can include inciting others to attempt to overthrow the government, belonging to an organization advocating the violent overthrow of the government, or publishing any material calling for violent revolution: "The man was accused of *sedition* because of his membership in a Marxist organization."

Treason is an attempt to overthrow one's own government by any means, especially by betrayal to a foreign government, as when one gives aid and comfort to an enemy: "While trying to overthrow one's government is *treason*, simply expressing disagreement with the government is not *treason*, though some nations have made public criticism of the government illegal."

SELF-INTERESTED/SELFISH (ADJ.)

A *self-interested* action is done to satisfy a desire of the self and may or may not unacceptably treat or ignore others: "Exercising regularly is a *self-interested* behavior."

A *selfish* action (when distinguished from a *self-interested* one) unacceptably treats others for the agent's own purposes: "Refusing to put down one's lunch long enough to throw a rope to some guy who's drowning is pretty *selfish*."

SENSUAL/SENSUOUS (ADJ.)

Sensual normally implies the gratification of the senses or the indulgence of physical appetites. *Sensual*, unlike *sensuous*, often carries an unfavorable connotation, suggesting grossness or lewdness. *Sensuous* can mean "characterized by the gratification of the senses, having strong sensory appeal, or characterized by sense impressions or imagery aimed at the senses." *Sensuous* often also implies gratifying the senses for the sake of aesthetic pleasure: "The refined aristocrat enjoyed the *sensuous* music of Wagner and the poetry of Dickinson, but his self-indulgent friend was given to debauchery and other *sensual* indulgences."

SENTIMENT/SENTIMENTALITY (N.)

A *sentiment* suggests an opinion based on emotion or feeling rather than reason: "Her *sentiments* about religion haven't changed since childhood."

Sentimentality can refer to a sentimental idea, but its usual application is to what is excessively or affectedly emotional: "We wanted honest, appropriate emotion from him, but he gave us distasteful *sentimentality*."

SENTINEL/SENTRY (N.)

A *sentinel* is a guard or *sentry*, but a *sentry* designates a soldier posted to prevent the passage of unauthorized persons: "The veteran was a *sentry* in the military and now works as a *sentinel* for a bank."

SERF/SLAVE/VASSAL (N.)

A *serf* was a member of the lower classes in feudal systems, bound to the land and subject to the will of the landowning lord. *Slave* describes a person bound in servitude as the property of another. A *serf's* status resembled that of a *slave*, except that the lords had certain responsibilities toward the *serfs*, and the *serfs* would stay but the lords would go when the land was sold: "Because *serfs* and their families were bound to a particular area of land, they were at times less likely to be split up than *slaves*, who were treated as chattel or movable property."

In the medieval pecking order, a *vassal* enjoyed a somewhat higher rank than that of a *serf*. *Vassals* were tenant farmers permitted to hold and work land, provided that they helped support and pledged allegiance to a lord. In modern usage, a *vassal* can be applied to anyone subject to another's controlling influence: "Most Hollywood actors and actresses in the 1940s were *vassals* of the studios."

SEWAGE/SEWERAGE (N.)

Sewage is the waste flowing through *sewerage*—the pipes, pumps, sewers, and treatment plants: "Although we upgraded our city's *sewerage*, no one has been able to improve *sewage*."

SHOVEL/SPADE (N.)

Shovels, which often move dirt, coal, or snow, are tools with long handles and broad scoops: "We used a *shovel* to remove the snow from the walk."

Although a *shovel* can be used for digging, that task is especially suitable for *spades*, whose rounded blades make digging easier. Further, the top of a *spade* is shaped to fit a foot pressed against it: "We used the *spade* to dig the hole."

SICK/SICKLY (ADJ.)

People who are ill are *sick*; those who are habitually or frequently ill are *sickly*: "Everyone becomes *sick* periodically, but some children have the misfortune of growing up *sickly*."

SIMPLE/SIMPLISTIC (ADJ.)

What is *simple* has few features or parts, is plain and unadorned, is easy to understand, or is easy to use: "The potato chip clip, designed to keep bags of chips sealed, is *simple* in every sense."

What is *simplistic* is shallow or excessively *simple*: "We won't waste time on any *simplistic* remedies."

SKETCH/SKIT (N.)

The terms *sketch* and *skit* are sometimes used interchangeably. Nevertheless, in theatrical presentations, a *sketch* is either a serious playlet that is often improvised or a playlet in a revue or variety show, while a *skit* is a short comical piece: "The *sketch* contained the acting portion of the revue." "Each episode of *Saturday Night Live* contains musical performances and *skits.*"

SKILLED/SKILLFUL (ADJ.)

Although there are contexts in which the two words are interchangeable, *skilled* usually implies long experience or special training: "We need more *skilled* workers."

Skillful implies natural ability, which may be refined: "The man had always been a *skillful* athlete, even as a young boy."

SLIT/SLOT (N.)

A *slit* is any opening, such as a cut, tear, or crack, that is long, straight, and narrow: "We just noticed the *slit* in her dress."

A *slot* is a narrow groove or opening, such as the groove for receiving coins in a vending machine: "Please put the coin into the *slot.*"

SPECIOUS/SPURIOUS (ADJ.)

Anything *specious* looks or sounds good, true, or valid but isn't: "A *specious* argument can mislead people."

Anything *spurious* is ungenuine or counterfeit, including something forged or intentionally deceptive: "The supervisor realized that the worker was giving a *spurious* excuse."

SPEED/VELOCITY (N.)

Speed refers to how fast a body is moving, without regard to the direction of the movement: "If we increase our driving *speed*, we'll decrease gas mileage."

Velocity refers to the rate of change of position along a straight line in relation to time. Technically, *velocity* involves both *speed* and direction: "We wanted to know the *velocity* of the bullet between two points."

SPIRE/STEEPLE (N.)

A *spire* is a slender, tapering object atop a tower. A *steeple* is a tower rising above a building, often a church. In short, a *spire* crowns a *steeple*: "The *steeple* was supermounted by a *spire*."

SPRAIN/STRAIN (N.)

A *sprain* is a wrenching or tearing of the ligaments holding a joint together: "The *sprain* of his ankle involved pain and swelling."

A muscular *strain* or pulled muscle is an overstretching of a muscle: "Because he lifted too much weight at the gym, he developed a *strain*."

STABLE/STALL (N.)

A *stable* is a building where animals, such as horses or cows, are sheltered; a *stall* is a compartment for an animal, though other structures such as public restrooms also have *stalls*: "After we entered the *stable*, we saw the horse's *stall*."

STALACTITE/STALAGMITE (N.)

Stalactite (Greek for "that which drips") is a deposit of calcium carbonate and other minerals precipitated from mineralized water solutions: "The *c* in *stalactite* reminds us that it hangs from the *c*eiling of limestone caves." *Stalactites* can also be attached to cave walls.

If the mineral deposit rises from the ground of a limestone cave, it is a *stalagmite*: "The *g* in *stalagmite* reminds us that it hangs from the ground of limestone caves."

STAMMER/STUTTER (N.)

A *stammer* is an involuntary pause or stop in speech: "Her *stammer* was due to her fear of public speaking."

A *stutter* is a rapid repetition of sounds: "The man's *stutter* was not due to momentary fear but to a speech disorder."

STRATAGEM/STRATEGY/TACTICS (N.)

A *stratagem* is a plan or trick intended to deceive, or a cleverly contrived scheme or maneuver for achieving an end: "The robber's feigning illness was a *stratagem* for getting inside the building."

Strategy refers to the overall planning and directing of large-scale operations, with an eye toward long-range goals. In military usage, *strategy* implies planning major operations intended to win a war or achieve its major objectives: "The *strategy* of invading on every front was successful in winning the war."

Tactics are the actions and maneuvers necessary to achieve short-term objectives, as well as the means of carrying out a *strategy*: "The general asserted that *tactics* win battles, and *strategy* wins wars."

STUPOR/TORPOR (N.)

A *stupor* is a state of heaviness when the mind is deadened, as by extreme drowsiness, alcohol or opiates, or the coma of disease. Any state ranging from a dream-like trance to almost complete unconsciousness can be a *stupor*: "His *stupor* was from opium."

A *torpor* is a condition of suspended animation resembling dormancy or hibernation, a state devoid of feeling and exertion: "Known for her previously active body and mind, the sickly, elderly woman was now heavily medicated and lying in a deathlike *torpor*."

SUNBLOCK/SUNSCREEN (N.)

Sunblocks work by physically deflecting ultraviolet (UV) rays and include zinc oxide and titanium dioxide: "Although *sunblocks* used to be thick and conspicuous (like the goopy white stuff on lifeguards' noses), they now blend into the skin better."

Sunscreens work by chemically filtering UV rays, and while they used to absorb only UV-B rays, they can now absorb UV-A rays, too: "Most *sunscreens*, whether creams, lotions, or gels, are transparent when applied."

SWEET POTATO/YAM (N.)

Sweet potatoes are the orange roots of the morning glory (*Ipomoea batatas*), whereas *yams* are brownish starchy tubers (underground outgrowths of the stem) of the vines of the genus *Dioscorea*: "Although *sweet potatoes* and *yams* may have a similar taste, they are distinct vegetables."

T

TESTAMENT/WILL (N.)

A *testament* is the section of a *will* that deals solely with the disposition of property: "The billionaire's *testament* was complex because of the amount of property involved."

A *will* is the legal statement of a person's wishes concerning the disposal of his or her estate and of other matters to be performed after death: "The *will* included directions about the funeral and the nature of the burial."

TESTY/TOUCHY (ADJ.)

A *testy* person is one whose irascibility (quickness to anger) is occasioned by petty annoyances: "The *testy* supervisor would fume over the smallest annoyance."

A *touchy* person is both excessively inclined to take personal offense and overly sensitive: "The *touchy* customer was offended when his server wasn't devoting all her time to him."

THWACK/WHACK (V.)

To *thwack* is, perhaps onomatopoetically, to hit or strike vigorously with something flat: "She *thwacked* her husband with the flat of her hand."

To *whack* is to strike a smart, resounding blow: "The professional wrestler Edward 'Wahoo' McDaniel would *whack* wrestlers with his 'tomahawk chop.' "

TIDAL WAVE/TSUNAMI (N.)

A *tidal wave* is a swell of cresting water due to the gravitational effect of the moon, sometimes magnified by strong winds. Technically, the expression *tidal wave* should be applied to the crest of a tide as it moves around Earth. The term *tidal bore* is also used to describe the wavelike upstream rush of water caused by the incoming tide: "*Tidal waves* don't typically affect water deeper than thirty feet."

A *tsunami* (Japanese for "harbor wave") is a series of ocean waves generated by submarine movements, which can be caused by earthquakes, volcanic eruptions, landslides beneath the ocean, or even meteorites. In open oceans, *tsunamis* can have wavelengths of up to several hundred miles and travel at speeds of hundreds of miles per hour, and yet have heights of less than three feet, permitting them to pass unnoticed beneath a ship: "*Tsunamis* occur principally in the Pacific Ocean after shallow-focus earthquakes registering more than 6.5 on the Richter scale."

TIMID/TIMOROUS (ADJ.)

Timid people lack self-confidence, and their shyness causes them to avoid difficult situations. Because of their lack of courage, *timid* people tend to be overcautious, avoiding change and uncertainty: "The *timid* investor was opposed to any risk taking."

Timorous people tend to be dominated more by

extreme fear than by extreme caution and tend to shrink from action requiring independence or self-assertion: "The boy was so *timorous* that he would rarely leave his house except for school."

TINGE/TINT (N.)

A *tinge* is a small amount of color incorporated or added: "The chutney and other relishes gave the food a yellowish *tinge*."

A *tint* is a shade of a color, especially a pale or delicate one: "Pastel shades are also known as *tints*."

TOUPEE/WIG (N.)

A *toupee* is a partial wig designed to cover a bald spot: "The man wore a *toupee* to cover the crown of his head."

A *wig* is a headpiece of artificial hair: "The bald man decided to wear a *wig*."

TRACE/VESTIGE (N.)

Both *trace* and *vestige* indicate what has existed or happened. *Trace*, the more common word, is derived from Latin *tractus* ("a dragging"). It applies to any evidence, such as a footprint, a fragment, a track, or a lingering odor, that suggests the prior existence or presence of something: "There was a *trace* of her perfume in the bedroom."

A *vestige*, a word with fewer uses, is a slight but actual indication of something that no longer exists: "After neglecting his body and health for decades, this former athlete is a *vestige* of his former self."

TRAITOROUS/TREACHEROUS (ADJ.)

People are *traitorous* to nations. *Traitorous* implies actual treason or a serious betrayal of trust to a nation: "The *traitorous* general was hanged."

Treacherous, a word of wider application, implies both a readiness to betray trust, when applied to persons, and a disposition to lead to peril or disaster because of delusive appearances, when applied to things: "The ice made the road *treacherous*."

TRAMP/VAMP (N.)

When applied to women, a *tramp* is a prostitute or a woman regarded as promiscuous: "The girl's prudish mother called her a *tramp* simply because she had had three boyfriends within four years."

A *vamp* is an unscrupulous flirt, who uses her charms to entrap and exploit men: "The *vamp* used her charms to persuade men to pay her bills."

TRANSIENT/TRANSITORY (ADJ.)

What is *transient* lasts or stays only briefly: "Those apartments aren't rented to *transient* renters."

Although *transitory* is a synonym of *transient*, the former often emphasizes the changeability of things: "Fame in Hollywood is *transitory*."

TRIUMPHAL/TRIUMPHANT (ADJ.)

Triumphal applies to commemorating or celebrating victories, whereas *triumphant* means "victorious" or "rejoicing in victory or success": "The *triumphal* procession was honoring the *triumphant* warriors."

TRUSTEE/TRUSTY (N.)

A *trustee* is an appointed or elected member of a board, who directs the funds and policies of an institution: "The *trustees* of the university voted to add a wing to the student center."

A *trusty* is a convict granted special privileges: "The *trusty* was given keys to rooms to which most prisoners would have no access."

TUMULT/TURMOIL (N.)

A *tumult* is a din or commotion produced by a crowd, though it can also be mental or emotional agitation: "The immediate stimulus for the vandalism and *tumult* was a loss by the local football team."

Turmoil is extreme confusion and agitation from any cause: "The country was in *turmoil* after the assassination of its president."

TWERP/TWIT (N.)

A *twerp* is an insignificant, contemptible person: "The rude *twerp* was ejected from the town hall after he continued to interrupt the meeting."

A *twit* is a foolishly annoying person or simply a fool: "No one enjoyed listening to the complaints and demands of the town's most notorious *twit*."

TYPHOID (TYPHOID FEVER)/TYPHUS (N.)

Typhoid (or *typhoid fever*) is so named because its symptoms resemble those of *typhus*, a different disease. *Typhoid fever*, caused by the bacteria *Salmonella typhi*, is most commonly transmitted by food or water contaminated by feces from infected persons. It is an acute infectious disease, the symptoms of which can include high fever, profuse sweating, gastroenteritis, cough, headache, and delirium: "Most Americans who get *typhoid fever* get it when traveling abroad and consuming infected food or drink."

Typhus applies to diseases caused by any various species of rickettsiae, a form of bacteria. *Typhus* is transmitted by the bites of fleas, mites, or ticks from infected rodents (particularly rats). The disease is marked by high fever, stupor alternating with delirium, intense headache, and a dark red rash: "Anne Frank died of *typhus* in the Bergen-Belsen concentration camp."

${\mathcal{U}}$

UNEXCEPTIONABLE/
UNEXCEPTIONAL (ADJ.)

Anything *unexceptionable* is completely satisfactory—that is, something to which there is no reasonable objection: "Her statements were *unexceptionable* but unfortunately bland."

Anything *unexceptional* is ordinary and unremarkable: "It is usually more difficult to recall and describe an *unexceptional* person than one who has features making him stand out."

USABLE/USEFUL (ADJ.)

What is *usable* is capable of being used; what is *useful* is helpful, beneficial, or advantageous: "An uncomfortable pen with little ink may be temporarily *usable* without being particularly *useful*."

USAGE/USE (N.)

Usage designates either the act of using something or, as in linguistic *usage*, accepted, customary, or habitual practice. *Usage*, in its prescriptive sense, suggests practices that have been so common for so long that they serve to guide what is widely considered appropriate: "Commonly used linguistic forms among the most literate speakers and writers carry weight as embodying standards of *usage*."

Use can designate many things, such as the act of using, a particular service, or what something is used for: "She put her knowledge to good *use*."

USE/UTILIZE (V.)

Although there may be contexts in which the two are interchangeable, careful usage favors *use* when meaning "to put into action or service" and *utilize* when meaning "to make practical, productive, or worthwhile use of": "Because we had no bleach to *use*, we decided to *utilize* a mixture of lime and water to clean the walls."

V

VACANT/VACUOUS (ADJ.)

Both *vacant* and *vacuous* designate things that lack content. What is *vacant* lacks what it appropriately or normally contains, such as an occupant, a tenant, or an inmate. The word *vacant* usually applies to physical things, with a few exceptions (a *vacant* look): "We rented the last *vacant* room."

What is *vacuous* exhibits the absolute emptiness of a vacuum. In its literal use, *vacuous* can describe a globe of an incandescent lamp. In its figurative and perhaps more common use, *vacuous* can describe minds, looks, or expressions: "His mind was so *vacuous* that he seemed incapable of even one insightful thought."

VENAL/VENIAL (ADJ.)

A *venal* person is corruptible, as one open to bribery: "The drug trafficker offered a bribe to the *venal* customs agent."

What is *venial* is easily excused, forgiven, or pardoned: "We agreed that his not offering me some of the pie was, at worst, a *venial* sin."

VERBIAGE/VERBOSITY (N.)

Both *verbiage* and *verbosity* describe the use of excessive words. *Verbiage*, though, normally applies to what is written; and *verbosity*, primarily to spoken speech. What's more, *verbiage*, in contrast to *verbosity*, often suggests obscureness or even meaningless: "The professor's pedantic *verbosity* was boring but at least intelligible— unlike his meaningless *verbiage*, which we had to read."

VIGOR/VIM/VITALITY (N.)

Vigor emphasizes strength from a fundamentally sound and active mind or body: "Triathletes must have extraordinary *vigor* for meeting mental and physical demands."

Vim emphasizes the display of extraordinary energy put to work: "When Napoleon was next to his soldiers, they were inspired and fought with *vim*."

Although *vitality* can be used literally as simply the capacity to live, grow, or develop, it often designates outstanding mental or physical energy or *vigor*: "We were impressed by the *vitality* that the elderly gardener displayed."

W

WARP/WEFT/WOOF (N.)

A *warp* is the series of yarns placed lengthwise in a loom and crossed by the horizontal yarns, called the *weft* or *woof*: "The yarn constituting the *warp* is perpendicular to the *weft*, or *woof*."

WASTAGE/WASTE (N.)

Wastage is loss through legitimate use, as through wear, leakage, decay, or deterioration: "Baseball bats that are used regularly will start to show signs of *wastage* and will need to be replaced."

Waste is often a result of careless use or consumption, though it can simply describe the product of a process, such as trash or excrement: "Although the *waste* of resources is deplorable, *wastage* is inevitable."

WATERPROOF/WATER-RESISTANT (ADJ.)

What is *waterproof* prevents water from entering; it is impervious to water. What is *water-resistant* repels water for a time but isn't completely *waterproof*: "For deep-sea diving, we needed *waterproof* equipment, not simply *water-resistant* equipment."

WHIM/WHIMSY (N.)

A *whim* is a sudden or capricious idea or an arbitrary thought or impulse: "He parachuted out of a plane on a *whim*."

Whimsy can refer to an odd or fanciful idea but especially applies to humorous objects or creations, particularly in art or literature: "The author's intellect and free-flowing imagination enabled him to produce both serious literature and *whimsy*."

WHIRL/WHORL (N.)

A *whirl* is the shape of something rotating or circling rapidly or simply a confused movement (a *whirl* of work): "We couldn't help noticing the *whirl* of the spinning top."

A *whorl* is something coiled, spiral, or circular in appearance: "In fingerprinting, a *whorl* is a complete circle of ridge shapes rather than a loop or an arch." "We saw a *whorl* of smoke rise from the chimney."

WOEBEGONE/WOEFUL (ADJ.)

Woebegone applies to what is affected with or marked by deep sorrow, grief, dejection, or defeat. A person with a *woebegone* expression is someone so transparently and demonstrably sad and dejected that observers may also feel sad just by looking at the person: "The *woebegone* man at our dinner party appeared so dejected that we couldn't enjoy our dinner."

Woeful is literally "full of woe"—that is, sad and mournful—though the word can also mean "causing woe" and "deplorably bad" (a *woeful* performance): "The child's eyes gave her a *woeful* expression."

X

X-AXIS/Y-AXIS (N.)

On a graph, the *x-axis* runs horizontally across the page, whereas the *y-axis* runs vertically: "To remember that the *x-axis* is horizontal and the *y-axis* is vertical, you need only remember that an uppercase *Y* has a vertical bar."

X CHROMOSOME/Y CHROMOSOME (N.)

The *X chromosome* and *Y chromosome* are sex-determining chromosomes in human beings and in many animals: "A normal human female has two *X chromosomes*, whereas a normal human male has one *X chromosome* and one *Y chromosome*."

Y

YIN/YANG (N.)

Yin is the feminine passive principle in nature, which in Chinese cosmology is revealed in darkness, cold, or wetness and which combines with *yang*, the masculine active principle revealed in light, heat, or dryness: "The combination of *yin* and *yang* is thought to produce all that comes to be."

YOUNG/YOUTHFUL (ADJ.)

Young is factual, describing whatever has lived or existed only a short time: "The six-year-old was too *young* to understand fully the concept of divorce."

Youthful is normally restricted to human beings and usually suggests the attractive qualities of youth, such as freshness and vitality, though it can occasionally refer to inexperience and immaturity (a *youthful* indiscretion): "One can have a *youthful* appearance without being *young*."

Z

ZEAL/ZEST (N.)

Zeal is keen and possibly even fanatical interest in pursuing something, especially a cause or an idea: "We were impressed by the *zeal* with which she pursued her cause."

Zest refers to vigorous and enthusiastic enjoyment, as well as an exciting or piquant quality: "The enthusiastic man was never bored but displayed a *zest* for life."

SELECTED BIBLIOGRAPHY

The American Heritage Dictionary of the English Language. 3rd ed. Boston: Houghton Mifflin, 1992.

Bernstein, Theodore. *The Careful Writer: A Modern Guide to English Usage.* New York: Atheneum, 1973.

Fowler, H. W. *A Dictionary of Modern English Usage.* Scranton, Pa.: Hadden Craftsmen, 1944.

Garner, Bryan A. *Garner's Modern American Usage.* New York: Oxford University Press, 2003.

Gause, John T. *The Complete University Word Hunter.* New York: Thomas Y. Crowell, 1967.

Graham-Barber, Lynda. *Toad or Frog, Swamp or Bog? A Big Book of Nature's Confusables.* New York: Four Winds Press, 1994.

Green, John, Maggie Koerth, Chris Connally, and Christopher Smith. *Mental Floss: What's the Difference?* New York: Collins, 2006.

Linfield, Jordan L., and Joseph Krevisky. *Word Traps.* New York: Innovation Press, 1993.

Nobleman, Marc Tyler. *What's the Difference?* New York: Barnes & Noble, 2005.

Partridge, Eric. *Usage and Abusage.* Middlesex, UK: Penguin, 1974.

Paxson, William C. *The New American Dictionary of Confusing Words.* New York: Signet, 1990.

Phythian, B. A. *A Concise Dictionary of Confusables: All Those Impossible Words You Never Get Right.* New York: John Wiley, 1990.

Room, Adrian. *Dictionary of Confusable Words.* Chicago: Fitzroy Dearborn Publishers, 2000.

Room, Adrian. *Dictionary of Confusing Words and Meanings.* London: Routledge & Kegan Paul, 1985.

Room, Adrian. *Dictionary of Contrasting Pairs.* New York: Routledge, 1988.

Room, Adrian. *Room's Dictionary of Differences.* New York: Everest House Publishers, 1982.

Rovin, Jeff. *What's the Difference? A Compendium of Commonly Confused and Misused Words.* New York: Ballantine, 1994.

Shaw, Harry. *Dictionary of Problem Words and Expressions.* New York: McGraw-Hill, 1975.

Soucie, Gary. *What's the Difference Between Apes and Monkeys and Other Living Things?* New York: John Wiley, 1995.

Soucie, Gary. *What's the Difference Between Lenses and Prisms and Other Scientific Things?* New York: John Wiley, 1995.

Urdang, Laurance. *The Dictionary of Confusable Words.* New York: Ballantine, 1988.

Webster's New Dictionary of Synonyms. Springfield, Mass.: Merriam-Webster, 1984.

Webster's Third New International Dictionary of the English Language. Springfield, Mass.: G. & C. Merriam, 1971.

Rod L. Evans, Ph.D., teaches philosophy at Old Dominion University in Norfolk, Virginia. He is the author or coauthor of fifteen books, including *The Gilded Tongue*, *The Right Words*, *Getting Your Words' Worth*, and *Every Good Boy Deserves Fudge: The Book of Mnemonic Devices*.